BEYOND MAJORITY RULE

voteless decisions in the
Religious Society of Friends

MICHAEL J. SHEERAN, S.J.
Regis College, Denver, Colorado

Permission to reprint must be
obtained in writing from:
Book Services Committee
Philadelphia Yearly Meeting
1515 Cherry Street
Philadelphia, Pennsylvania 19102

Printed in the United States
by Graphics Standard, Inc., West Chester, Pennsylvania

Cover design by Sue L. LaPenta

This book is dedicated to my father,
Leo J. Sheeran.

About the Author

Michael Sheeran is a Jesuit priest who became interested in the Religious Society of Friends in 1968 when he was studying religious communities which practice communal discernment, a decision making process which the Jesuit Order also utilized when it was founded in 1540 but lost within a generation. During doctoral work in the Department of Politics at Princeton University, he returned to the topic, spending two years conducting interviews, reading, and participant observation focused on the communal discernment tradition as it is exemplified in the voteless decisions of Quakers in Philadelphia Yearly Meeting.

Born in New York City in 1940, Michael Sheeran entered the Society of Jesus at Florissant, Missouri, in 1957. Since then, he has taught at Midwestern Jesuit high schools and colleges. Currently Vice President for Academic Affairs at Regis College in Denver, Colorado, he spends his free hours in teaching individuals how to pray and helping groups to make decisions through a common search for religious peace, a process which carries them beyond majority rule into communal discernment.

Contents

Foreword

Quaker scholars like Caroline Stephen, Rufus Jones, Howard Brinton, Hugh Doncaster and Elton Trueblood have written helpful accounts of the decision making process that takes place in the Quaker meeting for business. But even in this ecumenical age it is something new to see ourselves mirrored, in the process of making group decisions, in this penetrating study that has been made by a Jesuit scholar, Michael J. Sheeran.

Having selected Philadelphia Yearly Meeting as his scene of focus and possessing an extensive knowledge of the history of the Religious Society of Friends, Michael Sheeran, over a period of two years (1973-75), had a chance to observe the actual process of decision making by visiting a wide range of local monthly meetings as well as annual yearly sessions of the Philadelphia Yearly Meeting. He also talked personally on the intricacies of the decision making process with Quakers in both the Philadelphia and New Jersey areas. At many points his telling anecdotes, and the searching queries that he raises in this lively sketch of contemporary decision making, indicate that he may well know us better than we know ourselves!

In 1977 his study was submitted to the faculty of the Graduate School of Princeton University for a doctorate in politics and received its high commendation. Philadelphia Yearly Meeting of Friends, wishing to share this excellent study more widely, has encouraged its publication.

The initial third of the study, together with a sizable appendix, is devoted to a historical account of the first half-century of Quakerism in Britain and to its religious forerunners. Michael Sheeran selects with approval words from Thomas K. Brown: "The meeting for business is in essence, the meeting for worship focussed on specific matters." In his early chapters he describes with great care the meeting for worship and the experience of the Divine Presence that may come in the corporate waiting silence or in the vocal ministry that may grow out of that silence. It is out of the experience of the Presence in the midst that witness comes to the guidance that is to be found there and to the inner call for obedience to its direction.

Pope John XXIII once told of how in the first week after his consecration as Pope he could not sleep. He seemed crushed by the realization of his responsibility for the care of well over half a billion souls. At the close of the week he finally fell asleep and dreamed that the Lord approached him and, using his new name said: "Giovanni, what in the world is the matter with you with this no-sleeping business? Do you think you are in this thing alone?" After that Pope John reported that he had no more trouble sleeping!

In the experience of the early Quakers, it was ever so clear to them that they were not "in this thing alone." In their local meeting for worship, they found a Presence and a Guide that over and over again confirmed for them Isaac Penington's piercing words: "There is that near you which will guide you. O Wait for it and be sure that ye keep to it" (99th Letter). When these local meetings for worship were charged with carrying out a monthly meeting for business, the mood of the meeting for worship, the openness for guidance and the close dependence and trust of each other went with it. Such a monthly meeting for business carried out the social responsibilities that were entrusted to it. There was the care of the families of Quakers who were in prison or whose property had been seized; the keeping of records of "sufferings" imposed on Quakers by the persecutions; the handling of the admission of new members; the care of marriages and burials; and even of dealing with any misconduct or any laxity in carrying out the Quaker testimonies. Such meetings also provided a committee of clearness in which personal leadings and concerns could be shared and if unity with them was found, they could be encouraged and given any needed support.

No matter how earthy the matters to be decided might be in such a corporate exercise of decision making as the meeting for business, it was never to lose its spiritual nature. In an epistle written from Worcester prison on January 30, 1675, George Fox made clear that at their meeting for business "Friends are not to meet like a company of people about town or parish business, neither in their men's or women's meetings, but to wait upon the Lord." William Braithwaite in his *Second Period of Quakerism* writes, "Every business meeting was concerned with knowing the mind of the Lord and sought to guide the action by the weight of spiritual judgment rather than by mechanical counting of heads or the rhetorical and argumentative skill of the speaker" (p. 278). In another telling paragraph William Braithwaite sums up the ultimate thrust of these local meetings for worship and business carried on as they were by ordinary Quaker farmers, artisans and traders: "The quiet meetings resolutely maintained up and down the land, remained the centers of power and offered an invincible resistance to persecution . . . . By holding meetings through storms of persecution with unflinching tenacity, publicly and with open doors, Friends not only secured the continuance of their own Society but greatly contributed to the preservation of Non-Conformity as a whole."

In the closing pages of his account of early Friends, Michael Sheeran, in spite of his spirited defense of the necessity for centralizing the powers of Quaker governance in the closing decades of the seventeenth century, admits that it is in these earlier local monthly meetings that he found the decisive clues for the uniqueness of the Quaker corporate decision making. For all of their frailty and their exaggerated notions of infallibility, they contained, in his judgment, the seed and the genius of authentic Quaker decision making. It is to their plumb line that he returns in the remaining two-thirds of his book that is devoted to the contemporary scene.

As intriguing as Michael Sheeran's account of the seventeenth century origins of the Quaker decision making process may be, it is the hundred tightly-packed pages that record his findings of its contemporary use that make the book a particular treasure. Convinced as he is that Friends have something of first importance to share in their technique of reaching a viable resolution of their own problems, in these chapters he has collected and analyzed dozens of striking examples that lay bare the presuppositions of the Quaker process.

These presuppositions have a double edge to them. On the one hand, they differentiate the process from the many attempts that writers like Frank Walser or Stuart Chase have made to discover a secular voteless concensus that might be detached from the spiritual element that marks the genuine Quaker decision making experience. On the other hand, these presuppositions warn contemporary Quakers that when they grow lax and fail to carry them out, the process breaks down and only shabby imitations of it remain.

I know of no comparable analysis of these presuppositions that compares with what Michael Sheeran has managed to present. There is in the beginning the necessity of having a group of limited size who know and respect and trust each other. Members of this group must be willing to listen to each other with open minds, to learn from each other and be willing to feel into the shaping of a decision that upon occasions might be drastically different from anything they had previously conceived. They must have experienced in their meetings for worship and in previous gatherings for decision making, that they are not "in this thing alone" but that given patience and sufficient openness there is a right resolution of the problem which they confront.

Along with this they must be assisted by a clerk whose qualities are radically different from an aggressive or a manipulative leader. The clerk, whom the group has themselves chosen, must be one who also knows that he or she is not "in this thing alone." They must be persons who have confidence in the process and trust that there is a right solution to be found. Clerks must have skill and patience and fairness and have such faith in the members of the group that they can receive their suggestions on the way to move and be able to formulate a minute that will finally meet with general approval without putting the matter to a vote. The process at its best presupposes that the clerk will not be hurried nor be "influenced by mere numbers or persistence . . . nor be hindered from making experiments by fear of undue caution nor prompted by novel suggestions to ill-considered courses." The clerk will listen with great care to "weighty Friends" but not give them undue attention.

Among the more common blockages to these presuppositions could be included: unwillingness on the part of members to attend Quaker business meetings regularly because of the danger of involvement in the carrying out of the decisions arrived at; unwillingness to come to such meetings with other then a fixed and unchangeable mind as to the outcome; unwillingness to lay aside pressure tactics to force an early decision; unwillingness to follow the Quaker caution "to use as few words as possible and as many as are necesary;" unwillingness to experience the communal togetherness that such an exercise involves; and unwillingness to be open for the transforming experience of a "covered" meeting which in silent periods in a meeting for business may take place. These are among the basic obstacles that contemporary Quakers must seek to correct if they are not to lose this treasure which they have inherited.

There is a modest but not especially convincing attempt in the closing chapters of the study to distinguish the "Christocentric" from the "Universalistic" Quakers in the Philadelphia Yearly Meeting and to see whether one group is more qualified than the other for carrying out the full dimensions of the decision making genius of the Quaker business meeting. His conclusion is that above all other qualifications is the question of whether the Friend, regardless of the theological formulation of faith, has in the meeting for worship or in the meeting for business actually experienced the Presence and felt what obedience to the Guide may mean. Earlier Sheeran had written: "Quakers do not begin with a theory. They begin with an *event*" (p. 5). This *event*, this knowing at first hand that the continuous revelation is still at work is, in his judgment, what really matters. It is at this point that he sees that the seventeenth century Friends and contemporary Friends, when they are authentic, are one.

Michael Sheeran might well have shared a passage here from his fellow Roman Catholic, Thomas Merton's experiential witness when he wrote: "You don't have to rush after it. It is there all the time. If you give it a chance, it will make itself known to you."

The gift of this study will search contemporary Friends to the core and our debt to Michael Sheeran is not small.

DOUGLAS V. STEERE

Preface

Roman Catholicism's Second Vatican Council urged Religious Orders to renew themselves by getting in touch with their roots. The Jesuit Order, of which the writer is a member, discovered in its earliest documents a forgotten decision making procedure called Communal Discernment. Members of the community were expected to share in decisions by praying about the issues the community faced, sharing with each other outcomes of the prayer, and moving through discussion and further prayer to virtually unanimous conclusions.

When Jesuits and other Catholic communities which share the Jesuit spiritual tradition began to implement Communal Discernment during the early 1970s, they found constant practical obstacles to success. In particular, lack of acceptance of the process, mistrust of other participants, and inability to put aside one's own interests seemed regular roadblocks.

A little more than a decade ago, this writer began to work with Catholic groups who were attempting to employ Communal Discernment in their major decisions. He decided to look for communities outside Catholicism which might have day-to-day experience with such a process. John C. Futrell, S.J., Director of Ministry Training Services in Denver, Colorado, suggested the Religious Society of Friends (Quakers), a small religious family of some two hundred thousand members worldwide who have utilized Communal Discernment—without using the name—as their ordinary decision making process for the past three centuries. Under the direction of Harry Eckstein and Walter F. Murphy, Professors of Politics at Princeton University, the writer undertook a doctoral dissertation on the Quakers, attempting to trace the origins and current practice of their voteless decisions. This book is a revision of that dissertation.

In addition to analysis of historical and contemporary Quaker sources, the study relies heavily upon interviews with about one hundred and fifty members of Philadelphia Yearly Meeting, the Quaker body selected for careful study. It would be foolhardy to attempt to thank all who were particularly helpful. Suffice it to say that the entire group of individuals who agreed to interviews, by their consideration and generous sacrifice of time, truly proved themselves Friends.

It is hoped that the book will be useful to Catholics and other Christians in tracing how Friends successfully employ a tradition of religious decision making which is deeply embedded in Scripture but which other Christians have typically lost. In particular, the ways Quakers seem to avoid the problems which faced Catholics new to the method are explored.

Social scientists and political philosophers are invited to discover in Quakers what may be the only modern Western community in which decision making achieves the group-centered decisions of traditional societies. In the Conclusion, the author discusses Friends as a possible answer to the common contemporary wish for advancement beyond the fragmented individuation of "liberal" man.

Finally, the author hopes Quakers themselves will find in these pages a helpful mirroring of Friends decision making. Newcomers to Quakerism and those who find themselves in roles of leadership within the community may find in this study an outsider's understanding of the possibilities and pitfalls of the Quaker method of going beyond majority rule.

M.J.S.

Denver, Colorado
September 1983

PART I

Historical

Chapter I

Quaker Beginnings, 1647–1666

The central idea was the complete elimination of majorities and minorities; it became the Quaker custom to reach all decisions in unity. The clerk of the meeting merely performed the function of reporting the corporate sense, i.e., the judgment of the assembled group, and of recording it. If there were differences of view, as there were likely to be in such a body, the consideration of the question at issue would proceed, with long periods of solemn hush and meditation, until slowly the lines of thought drew together towards a point of unity. Then the clerk would frame a minute of conclusion, expressing the "sense of the meeting."[1]

This simple decision making process already characterized the tiny Quaker communities which evolved after the first decade of explosive growth following 1647. In that year, as political England struggled towards the beheading of a king and declaration of Cromwell's commonwealth, which would occur two years later, George Fox began his effort to bring all the world to "walk in the light of Truth."[2] His greatest appeal would lie among England's Baptists, Seekers, Familists, Ranters, and other "masterless men" who together constituted the non-Episcopalian, non-Puritan politically insignificant 50 percent of the nation. At Fox's death, forty-four years later, one in every hundred Englishmen would be a Quaker,[3] and the process of replacing majority rule with unity would be firmly entrenched as the linchpin of this Quaker polity.

Central to the Quaker understanding of unity-based decision making is Fox's idea that there is "that of God in every one."[4] When a group of believers comes together to deliberate about the best way to serve God here and now, each expects to find in others some manifestation of "that of God," and looks for the mark of the Spirit of Christ—Truth with a capital "T"—in everyone else's remarks. In short, since the same Spirit speaks in each heart, the members expect to end their meetings united.[5]

But how were those meetings conducted? The earliest clear statement this writer has found is Edward Burrough's 1662 testimony concerning the origins of the London Business Meeting in 1655. Burrough tells us that those men who were not engaged in the full-time preaching and tract writing of the unordained ministers gathered every week or two to deliberate: "concerning providing convenient meeting places for the publishing of Truth; and how the poor people that believed should be honestly taken care for, that no want should be amongst them; and that the sick and weak and impotent should be visited and provided for; and that such servants as were put away out of their services for receiving the Truth, should be looked after, and placed in some honest employment."[6]

Their style of deliberation was singular, continues Burrough: "Not in the way of the world, as a worldly assembly of men, by hot contests, by seeking to outspeak and overreach one another in discourse, as if it were controversy between party and party of men, or two sides violently striving for dominion, in the way of carrying on some worldly interests for self-advantage; not deciding affairs by the greater vote, or the number of men, as the world, who have not the wisdom and power of God."[7]

The Quaker procedure is just the opposite, wrote Burrough: " . . . [I]n the wisdom, love and fellowship of God, in gravity, patience, meekness, in unity and concord, . . . and in the holy Spirit of truth, . . . in love, coolness, . . . as one only party, . . . to determine of things by a general mutual concord, in assenting together as one man in the spirit of truth and equity, and by the authority thereof."[8]

The Root of the Meeting for Business: Quaker Worship

As these remarks of Burrough make clear, early Friends understood the decision making dimension of Quaker life as one moment in the entire religious experience of the community. Today one is reminded forcefully of this fact by the five minutes or so of silent worship which begin and end every Quaker meeting for business. If one is to understand the Friends business meeting, it is necessary to appreciate the style of worship itself. The procedure is deceptively simple. All gather together in an unadorned room and sit in silent worship. After awhile, one or another

4

may stand and speak of a religious insight he or she feels called upon to share. The meeting ends, perhaps an hour after it began, with the general shaking of hands. An example of the power sometimes experienced in such a period of worship is reflected in Caroline E. Stephen's recollection of an 1872 meeting.

> On one never-to-be-forgotten Sunday morning, I found myself one of a small company of silent worshippers who were content to sit down together without words, that each one might feel after and draw near to the Divine Presence, unhindered at least, if not helped, by any human utterance. Utterance I knew was free, should the words be given; and before the meeting was over, a sentence or two were uttered in great simplicity by an old and apparently untaught man, rising in his place amongst the rest of us. I did not pay much attention to the words he spoke, and I have no recollection of their purport. My whole soul was filled with the unutterable peace of the undisturbed opportunity for communion with God.[9]

Robert Barclay, the Quaker Apologist, tells us:

> When I came into the *silent Assemblies* of God's people, I felt a *secret Power* among them, which touched my heart; and as I gave way unto it, I found the evil weakening in me, and the Good raised up. . . .
> Such is the evident certainty of that divine Strength, that is communicated by thus meeting together, and waiting in Silence upon God: that sometimes when one hath come in, that hath been unwatchful, and wandering in his Mind, or suddenly out of the hurry of outward business, and so not inwardly gathered with the rest; so soon as he retires himself inwardly, this Power being in a good measure raised in the whole Meeting, will suddenly lay hold upon his Spirit, and wonderfully help to raise up the Good in him, and beget him into the sense of the same Power, to the melting and warming of his Heart.[10]

In Fox's *Journal*, the most common observation of a Quaker meeting is to the effect that "we had a blessed meeting; the Lord's power and presence was felt among us."[11]

At the center of Quakerism is this communal *experience*. Quakers do not begin with a theory. They begin with an event in which, ideally, the presence of God is experienced by each person as part of a group experience. Rufus Jones emphasizes that "Quakerism is peculiar in being a group mysticism, grounded in Christian concepts." The experience is "mystical" in the extended sense of a "self-evident conviction" of the divine presence, a "vital discovery of divine Life revealing itself here and now in and through a group of persons who are bent on transmitting that Life."[12]

5

The entire Quaker format of worship, as described by Howard Brinton, can be understood best in terms of seeking this experience.

> At first sight, it might appear that the meeting can only be described by negatives—there is no altar, no liturgy, no pulpit, no sermon, no organ, no choir, no sacrament, and no person in authority. No external object of attention prevents the worshipper from turning inward and there finding the revelation of the Divine Will. Whatever is outward in worship must come as a direct result of what is inward—otherwise, it will be form without power. There must first be withdrawal to the source of power and then a return with power.[13]

Gerald K. Hibbert expresses the experiences in the language of sacrament:

> Suddenly or gradually we realise "the Presence in the midst," and the silence becomes fully sacramental. Thus comes the sense of our communion one with another through partaking together of the Bread of Life, and we go forth to actualise that communion and fellowship in our daily lives.[14]

In Quaker parlance, a special term is used to identify this phenomenon. During the time the group is aware of "the Presence in the midst," the meeting is "covered" or "gathered" or, in Barclay the Apologist's phrase, "gathered into the *Life*."[15]

Now the early meeting for business (a decision making meeting) is a type of meeting for worship, an outgrowth of the latter. It seeks to reach decisions "in the Life," decisions which grow out of the experience of God's invitations, his "leadings" during the time of gathered prayer. One might oversimplify, but only slightly, that the regular meeting for worship seeks corporately for God's presence; the special meeting for worship which focuses on matters of business seeks corporately for God's will. And, at least in serious matters, the group finds God's will by first finding God. The atmosphere of a meeting for business is well described by Richard Vann in a discussion on Buckinghamshire Monthly Meeting Minutes for 5 February 1683 in which the "extraordinary psychic atmosphere" requires that all present be in the "state and condition" of openness to God. Vann marvels at "this feeling that even one person out of harmony with the meeting could prevent it from accomplishing anything."[16]

The extraordinary authority credited to decisions made in this situation cannot be minimized. In the second part of this study we shall attempt to draw out the peculiar motivation to obey which is produced by the decision making rules of a unity-seeking body. Here let us underscore the enhancement of legitimacy which comes when a group believes that its decision is divinely guaranteed. Disobedience is not an act against the group, but sin against God himself. Even should a member be unable to see the wisdom of the decision some months after it was reached, he or she still feels weighty obligation to obey. Obedience is required whether he or she sees the reason or not, and must be obeyed until such time as the group is led to rescind the requirement, thus reflecting fresh divine guidance for new circumstances.

Individual Inspiration

At this point, we turn for a moment to a complementary Quaker belief. For, if the Spirit of God speaks to the meeting, he also speaks through individuals in the meeting. There is no reason to think that the Spirit's voice can be heard *only* in the gathered meeting. Let us see how individual inspirations (leadings) might occur and then turn to the community crises which sometimes arise out of them.

A typical example is the call of Marmaduke Stevenson: "In the beginning of the year 1655, I was at the plough in the east parts of Yorkshire; . . . and, as I walked after the plough, I was filled with the love and presence of the living God. . . . And . . . the word of the Lord came to me in a still, small voice, which I did hear perfectly, saying to me in the secret of my heart and conscience, 'I have ordained thee prophet unto the nations.' "

Stevenson accepted this call to missionary service. And "the Lord said unto me, immediately by His Spirit" that he would care for Stevenson's wife and children. With this reassurance, Stevenson and William Robinson set off for the American Colonies. As it turned out, the call was not only to mission but also to martyrdom; on October 27, 1659, both were hanged on Boston Common, the first Quakers to be executed under a 1658 Massachusetts statute against the "cursed sect" of Quakers.[17]

Revelation as Seed of Persecution, 1647–1649

Impressive as the missionary vocation and martyrdom of a Marmaduke Stevenson may be, such reliance on individual inspiration had its pitfalls. George Fox's own early experience of revelations illustrates the point well. For example, sometime in 1648, Fox had an "opening" "that such as were faithful to [God] in the power and light of Christ, should come up into that state in which Adam was before he fell, in which the admirable works of the creation, and the virtues thereof, may be known,

7

through the openings of that divine Word of wisdom and power by which they were made."[18]

Two important claims are made here. First, sinful man is capable of inner holiness, even perfection. Secondly, a man in that state of prelapsarian holiness can have direct and reliable divine revelation on the nature and qualities of all creation. So strong was Fox on the point that he even paused over "whether I should practise physic for the good of mankind, seeing the nature and virtues of the creatures were so opened to me by the Lord."[19]

This vision is the root of two prolonged difficulties. First, there was the claim that perfection is possible for man, a claim shared with General Baptists, Familists, and other sects. However, Fox expressed the claim in the language of the Ranters, an amorphous group of disenfranchised men notorious for their immoral lives. The Ranters simply carried Fox's idea of restoration to holiness a step further: If Christ's resurrection restores the believer to Adam's sinless state, then any action a believer performs, be it dancing or cursing or fornicating, is sinless! However, the Ranters would bring the Commonwealth's persecution on their heads in 1651 and 1652 when their leaders were imprisoned and the flock scattered into invisibility with religious groups similar to their own in theology among the "masterless men" of English society. Quakers would find themselves publicly suspect as being mere "externally upright Ranters" for more than a decade.[20]

The second prolonged difficulty with beginnings in this 1648 opening is more fundamental. Fox was proposing a theory of direct divine inspiration of an extraordinarily detailed sort: God showed him the inner workings of all reality. This divine illumination was dependent upon neither Book nor human event; hence, the normal avenues of independent verification were closed. Fox would spend decades trying to cope with the ramifications of this mystical experience. He would soon find that separate religious insights, at least when they are reduced to human concepts and language, can vary and can even contradict one another, yet he would have no adequate standard for assessing their validity. A religious community based on such sometimes conflicting openings would often find itself adrift. Fox first faced this central problem with the scandalous excesses of James Nayler.

The James Nayler Crisis, 1656

Certainly Marmaduke Stevenson's vocation and martyrdom was adequate to edify the community. But suppose a Friend's leading proves embarrassing. And suppose the Friend is a man of special prominence. James Nayler is a case in point. Well-known for his spirited and attractive presentation of Friends' beliefs, James Nayler vied with Fox himself as the most noteworthy Quaker during the period from 1652 to 1656. In an official narrative, London Yearly Meeting explains what occasioned the crisis:

> In 1655, Nayler came south to help in work in London, where he became ensnared by flatterers, who behaved themselves in an extravagant fashion, bowing, kneeling and singing before him. On going to Bristol he was persuaded by Friends there to see Fox, then in Launceston jail, but on the way he was taken and imprisoned at Exeter. He was freed in October, 1656, and a few days later entered Bristol on horseback with his followers around him. They spread garments before him and sang, "Holy, Holy, Holy, Lord God of Israel." The authorities interfered and sent him to London, where Parliament after long debates sentenced him to imprisonment after being whipped and pilloried in London and Bristol, and branded for a blasphemer, and having his tongue bored through.[21]

The seriousness of the problem that Nayler suddenly had become is illustrated by the fervor of Parliamentary debate. There had been previous messiahs in this religion-ridden age, such as William Franklin, Arise Evans, Theaureaujohn. All had been dealt with by local magistrates with brief prison terms. But to Nayler, Cromwell's House of Commons devoted six weeks of frenzied vitriol. The horrors Nayler finally suffered were an attempt to placate those who demanded a sentence of death. The difference? The other messiahs were insignificant men without serious followings. Nayler, however, was leader of a large movement which had spread rapidly, drawing many members from the anti-parliamentary Levellers and the immoral Ranters.[22]

Suddenly the pleadings in Quaker pamphlets for social justice began to look like preachments of political revolution. A 1653 publication had threatened, for example, that "the earth is the Lord's and the fullness thereof. He hath given it to the sons of men in general, and not to a few lofty ones which lord it over their brethren."[23] Another prophesied woe to "you lofty ones of the earth, who have gotten much of the creation into your hands . . . and are become lords of your brethren."[24]

"God is against you," Nayler himself told "covetous cruel oppressors who grind the faces of the poor and needy."[25] Elsewhere Nayler lamented, "Who could have believed that England would have brought forth no better fruits than these, now after such deliverance as no nation else can witness?"[26]

As the reader would expect, Nayler's case brought an increase of persecution upon the heads of Friends and a vivid sense of the vulnerability of the Quaker community to individual excess. In order to understand the significance of the Quaker response to this double threat, the reader is asked to consider Quaker organizational structures prior to the Nayler affair and then to contrast them with the changes Fox felt forced to introduce in its aftermath.

Early Quaker Polity, 1649–1656

In reporting the origin of Quaker meetings for business, George Fox comments: "The first Monthly Meeting was on this wise in the North: . . . we did meet concerning the poor, and to see that all walked according to the Truth, before we were called Quakers, about the middle of the nation in Nottinghamshire and Derbyshire, and part of Leicestershire, where there was a great convincement."[27]

These are all districts where Fox had found groups of adherents by the end of 1648, two years before Judge Hotham dubbed the sect Quakers. Since there are no records of the sessions held among these groups, we must turn to records of practice among the northern Seekers Fox attracted in 1652.[28]

In Westmoreland and East and West Riding, Fox found Seeker groups which already met at regular intervals of three or four weeks to handle relief of their poor and discipline of the "disorderly walkers" among their membership. In 1653, William Dewsbury, who had set up the East Riding Meeting the year before, wrote a general epistle urging that "one or two Friends who are most grown in the power and life, in the pure discerning in the Truth" should be chosen to "take care and charge over the flock of God" as overseers.[29]

In the same year, an epistle was sent out in Fox's name recommending various points of good order in the local business meetings. A secretary should keep a record of all "sufferings" which could eventually be shared with other Friends at a regional meeting. Idleness should be discouraged. Friends in financial straits should be aided if possible from locally collected and administered funds. Although it is clear that Fox and those who consulted with him prior to the letter's writing held great influence over the local meetings, it is equally clear that Fox was making strong suggestions to groups that were autonomous and self-governing. Constant encouragement was given to local resolution of problems. Provision, however, was made for special, regional gatherings for those instances

10

when local Friends were unable to resolve problems. But the very irregularity of such regional gatherings indicates how great was the primacy of the local meetings.[30]

It would appear that meetings for business were not held on a regular monthly basis in many districts outside the region; instead sessions might be summoned only when need was felt. With the increase of persecution, however, such gatherings became necessary on a more consistent basis. On one hand, those in jail and their families needed looking after, as did those who lost their employment because of joining Friends. On the other, any hint of immorality which might justify the persecutors' charge that Friends were "secret Ranters" must be remedied. The meetings kept busy discovering such "disorderly walkers;" they then either publicly asserted in writing that the individual in question was not a member of their group or obtained from the culprit a written public confession that his action had been contrary to "Friends' Principles" along with a promise of reformation. Both approaches were described as actions to "clear Truth."[31] For example, Fox notes in his *Journal* for 1655 that "Christopher Atkinson, that dirty man, had run out and brought dishonour upon the Lord's Truth and his name; but he was judged and denied by Friends, and he after gave forth a paper of condemnation of his sin and evil."[32]

By 1654, however, Fox had realized that regular local business meetings were important to the community's survival and had set about the task of "settling" Quaker groups where regularity was lacking.[33]

In that same year, Fox had gathered a sizable group of full-time itinerant preachers who, like himself, spread the Quaker good news about the Inner Light of Christ, establishing and then fortifying little groups of fellow believers wherever they travelled. The "Valiant Sixty" or "First Publishers of Truth," as they have come to be known in Quaker annals, taught a doctrine which can be summarized in four cardinal principles. There is:

(1) Something of divine origin—"that of God," "the Inner Light of Christ"—in every human being; (2) a universal grace; (3) a universal call to moral perfection and religious union with God; and (4) a continuing progressive revelation of God's will through the ages.[34]

The emphasis was not on specific doctrines about God, Christ, or redemption but on the kind of life that should be lived by someone who experiences God's activity in his life. Says British historian G. M. Trevelyan, "The finer essence of George Fox's queer teaching common to the excited

11

revivalists who were his first disciples was surely this: that Christian qualities matter much more than Christian dogmas."[35]

It is important to notice that, in this earliest period, Fox did almost nothing to organize his brethren above the local level. The meetings kept in touch with each other through the loose and informal contact of the Valiant Sixty or other travelling Friends. There is simply no indication that Fox or his followers had any more rigorous plan of governance in mind. As the reader is about to see, any development of polity above the local level seems always a step forced by the need to defend Friends from government actions or those inner excesses which invite government action; and always it is tailored to achieve maximum effect with a minimum of added structure.

Fox's Attempts to Protect Quaker Communities, 1656–1660

At the time of Nayler's punishment, George Fox, fresh out of jail, toured the nation and discovered an increase in the frequency of harassment for such Friendly offenses as refusal to pay tithes, take oaths, or show respect for civic officials by removing the hat. A significant explanation of increased persecution is, perhaps, found in Fox's remark, "Oliver Protector began to harden."[36]

Fox sought first to achieve a restoration of order within the various Friends' communities, bringing them back from "that evil spirit . . . which had drawn James Nayler and his followers out from Truth, to run Friends into heats about him."[37] He wrote three epistles to Friends, one urging that their "patience must get the victory and answer that of God in every one, must bring every one to it, and bring them from the contrary." This can be interpreted as a plea for internal reconciliation and, perhaps, a less "aggravating" public witness. The second and third epistles are concerned with deepening the sense of the Spirit's presence ("the power of the Lord") in meetings for worship and loving but firm guidance to be exercised by more mature Friends over those who may "go beyond their measure."

From this very positive starting point, Fox set out to reinforce the meagre structures of the separate communities: monthly meetings of men—prime places for discovering and dealing with "disorderly walkers"—were established wherever they were not already set up; special general meetings involving one or two representatives from each county were to be held at Skipton annually to bring ordinarily isolated local units together for a period of renewal and united decisions; "reliable" books were widely disseminated; and regional meetings were established to meet four times a year (quarterly meetings) throughout the nation.[38]

Fox did not use the Nayler episode to exercise undue personal power. He did, however, respond to the crisis by initiating a regular, if minimal, superstructure above the level of the local units. The local units remained primary, although the superstructure served to communicate and advise in a consistent way which the haphazard journeys of the travelling ministry—the First Publishers of Truth—had not been set up to achieve.[39]

The function of the now regular gatherings of travelling ministers and elders from local meetings was clearly regarded as advisory. There was no doubt of local sovereignty. An excellent illustration of the spirit with which the new structure would approach its task was the 1656 epistle of "the brethren in the north" which was sent from a special meeting of elders gathered at Balby. Since they wrote while Nayler's case was being debated in Parliament, their exhortations to internal discipline and self-constraint, including supervision by local elders, are understandable. But these Balby Friends followed their injunctions with a postscript that would set the tone for the regular gatherings of elders to follow.

> Dearly beloved Friends, these things we do not lay upon you as a rule or form to walk by, but that all, with the measure of light which is pure and holy, may be guided: and so in the light walking and abiding, these may be fulfilled in the Spirit, not from the letter, for the letter killeth, but the Spirit giveth life."[40]

The importance of Fox's tour of England becomes more apparent when we face the advisory nature of the Balby epistle and those that were to follow. Greater control over excesses could be exhorted by gatherings above the local level, but implementation was by local option. If the Balby proposals were to become effective, the vigorous charismatic presence of Fox was sometimes crucial. Fox's gentle but insistent efforts proved adequate to reunite and discipline the community after the Nayler fiasco, aided greatly, one must note, by Nayler's own humble repentance and return to the fold.

As for government opposition, it is not clear whether Christopher Hill has adequate evidence for his general judgment that "once the Nayler case had broken the radical-political back of Quakerism, the men of property seemed secure from the perils which had environed them since 1647."[41] That imprisonment of Quakers continued, there can be no doubt. Whether the pace slackened is hard to say.

It does seem clear that the tide of pamphlets from Quaker pens con-

13

tinued to urge social reform. Anthony Pearson advocated abolition of tithes as a device to relieve the poor. Already by 1658, John Audland prophesied immediate divine wrath against immoral Bristol—significantly, the town Nayler had entered as messiah two years previously and where he had subsequently been flogged the following year.[42]

The Restoration and Renewed Persecution

The turbulence immediately preceding the 1660 restoration of the monarchy brought forth a large volume of Quaker political tracts calling on Parliament to "set free the oppressed people." Army leaders were accused of arming Anabaptists and Quakers in an attempt to prevent the Restoration.[43]

The collapse of parliamentary government led Fox to personal despair over the political realm. Just before the Republic's fall, he issued an uncharacteristic pamphlet objecting to democracy itself. Its lengthy title expresses the theme: *A Few Plain Words To be considered by those of the Army, Or others that would have a Parliament That is chosen by the voyces of the people, to govern the three Nations. Wherein is shewed unto them according to the Scripture of Truth, that a Parliament so chosen are not likely to govern for God and the good of his People.*[44] This thoroughly anti-democratic essay still calls for abolition of tithes, reform of law, and religious toleration. It is also a prelude to the despair of politics that would take hold of Fox and his movement in 1660.[45]

When the Restoration finally occurred, suppression of Quakers by the agents of Charles II was singularly brutal.[46] One must remember that Quakers were among the most visible targets to be found by the Royalists in their drive to make the kingdom safe against Parliamentarianism and the "masterless men" who had joined the Army and who had otherwise supported the Parliamentary forces.

The Fifth Monarchy Uprising against the new king in early January 1661, led the government to mass imprisonment of Quakers as likely participants. Fox tells us that "several thousands" of Friends were imprisoned in January by the King and Council.[47]

At this point, Fox and Richard Hubberthorne drew up a declaration against "plots and fightings" to be presented to the king. It was seized while at the printer's and destroyed. A second version was prepared by Friends and printed over the names of Fox, Hubberthorne, and ten other prominent Quakers who wrote "in behalf of the whole body of the Elect People of God who are called Quakers." The king was told: "All Bloody

14

principles and practices, we as to our own particulars, do utterly deny, with all outward wars and strife and fightings with outward weapons, for any end or under any pretence whatsoever. And this is our testimony to the whole world."[48]

This is a curious document. A dozen prominent Friends took it upon themselves to declare that pacifism was a central Quaker tenet. Yet we know that at least two of the signers, Howgill and Hubberthorne, had advocated the use of force as late as 1659. And Fox, himself, though he had refused an army commission in 1651, still felt free in 1657 to urge "the inferior officers and soldiers" of the army to conquer Rome.[49] Further, it would appear that the plight of imprisoned Friends was so pressing that the twelve were led to define Quaker belief with an absoluteness uncharacteristic of the movement. Because their action—combined with the timely denial of Quaker complicity by Fifth Monarchy leaders just before their own execution[50]—brought relief from the large-scale imprisonment of Friends, it seems to have drawn no immediate objections from within the Quaker communities scattered over England.

But the action underscores the weakness of the position Friends were in. Conceived by their opponents as a national group of possibly revolutionary proclivity, they had no regular national unit which could speak authoritatively for them. To what extent was a declaration by twelve Friends—even twelve prominent ones—a definitive statement of the community's belief?

Even more important theoretically, if not recognized at the time, how could any body *representing* the local communities speak authoritatively for them all? The local autonomy which was central to Quaker communities implied a nondelegatable power of local decision. The Balby elders, in 1656, had gone as far as a nonlocal unit could go simply by giving strong advice to the local meetings. The proclamation of 1661 by the twelve leading Friends declared to the government a testimony of pacifism which not only had not been approved by all the local communities but which was inconsistent with the recent statements of some of the most prominent signers themselves. In this clear emergency, under great immediate threat of major persecution, the twelve had let necessity be their guide. Their action opened the door for Friends to metamorphose from a sect of locally sovereign communities to a church with central polity. This transition involved a substitution of central for local divine guidance.

For other sects, this substitution, though difficult, has not been fundamental because it does not affect the general body of doctrines the sect

15

holds. Not so for Friends. Quakerism is a religion which tries to be without doctrines. What is central instead is the common experience, the felt action of God in the gathered meeting. In the personal experience of decisions which arise from that felt presence, the Friend draws confidence that the decision is truly "of God" and therefore that it calls for his or her obedience. To transform this "authority from experience" into "authority from external directives" is to transplant a tree by cutting off its root. In fact, Friends will never quite make a successful transition from sect to church. The regional and national government units, no matter how justified in theory, remain in constant de facto tension with the theological fundamentum of experience which makes local meetings innately sovereign.[51]

But now back to 1661. Given Friends' high visibility and the government's efforts to suppress them, there was clear impetus for some sort of national structure in the early years after the Restoration. But the persecution was so strident that even those regular regional meetings Fox had succeeded in establishing in the 1656–1660 period[52] became irregular at best and disappeared entirely at worst.

The local communities, however, thrived in spite of the persecution. When others went into hiding, Friends insisted on meeting publicly for worship every First Day (Sunday). In some instances when all the parents in a meeting were imprisoned, their children kept the meeting going as usual. Says Christopher Hill, "One of the most important reasons for the survival of the Quakers was their stoutness under persecution, on which even their enemies commented."[53]

The Perrot Threat, 1661–1666

But in the midst of these once again isolated communities, an old problem emerged. Although James Nayler had died contrite and restored in 1660, his earlier heresy reemerged in the highly appealing John Perrot. Some writers have been so misled by the apparently paltry nature of Perrot's disagreement with Fox as to dismiss the issue as insignificant or even to blame Fox for being unduly harsh towards a relatively innocent offender.[54]

The occasion of the famous "hat controversy" was Perrot's leading in prayer that he should not remove his hat when he (or anyone else) prayed aloud in meeting for worship. This was an insight "which I have received by express commandment from the Lord God of heaven."[55] The reason Perrot's position was not insignificant is that it was a direct reminder of

Nayler's actions. Says Fox: "But James Nayler and some of them could not stay the meeting but kept their hats on when I prayed. And they were the first that gave that bad example amongst Friends."[56] Nor was Nayler's custom original. In a denunciation of hat-wearers in 1681, Fox indicates that this practice was a trademark of the Ranters: "And alsoe all such as weare their hatts when ffrinds pray, and are gotten into ye old rotten principle of ye ranters whoe sets up ye wearing theirof in oppostion to ye power of god."[57]

As one might expect, Perrot held a cluster of positions associated with Nayler and with the Ranters hidden within Quakerism and he numbered "most of those that had joyned to James [Nayler]" among his own enthusiasts.[58] At the center is the idea that the individual Friend should act according to his own leadings no matter what others may hold, even if one's leadings are exactly the opposite of the agreement of Friends. Perrot believed that: "The Lord in me [is] more worthy of audience and obedience than the voyce of any messenger to me; and therefore till I hear the voice of god in me, though I have heard the voice of a trumpet with me[,] I am to stand still and wait for a certain knowledge of the echoings through the valley of my soul, as found answerings of God's minde in me."[59]

Out of this doctrine came the anarchical argument that meetings for worship should not be scheduled regularly but should only occur when members of the community felt moved to worship together. Next Perrot imitated Nayler in growing a Jesus-like beard and encouraging a number of women to show him respect bordering on obeisance. Under color of achieving spontaneity, he organized separate evening worship sessions among London Friends. At this, Fox explicitly denounced the increasingly popular Perrot.[60] A pamphlet war ensued during the 1616–1665 period.

Perhaps the clearest statement of the basic threat which Perrot's thought presented is in Richard Farnsworth's 1663 critique. Farnsworth charged that Perrot first totally split the outward and inward man, then claimed that God's inner teachings touch only the inner man. Thus, the outward life need not be an expression of the inner convictions. For the old Ranters this had meant freedom from the need to live externally moral lives so long as their inner lives were renewed. For Perrot and his followers, it meant that one did enough if he conformed to the "outward" religious legislation of the restored and unFriendly king so long as he had a nonconforming heart. This was an all too appealing subterfuge to avoid being "liable to any persecutions of suffering for righteousness' sake."[61]

A good example of Perrot's technique may well be his own arrangement in 1662 to go into voluntary exile in Barbados in return for his release from Newgate Prison. This agreement was followed at once by his informing the Quaker settlement in Barbados that he was coming "to preach the Gospel" among them.[62]

To Fox, Perrot's journey to the New World did not have the earmarks of a divine mission.[63] For Perrot, this gap between inner life and outer expression seemed most acceptable. Once in Barbados, he divided his time between missionary journeys and taking on such unFriendly (but lucrative) duties as becoming royal negotiator to the neighboring Spanish (a post which involved wearing a sword) and acting as clerk of a court where Perrot cheerfully administered oaths.[64]

Chapter II

The Growth of Central Decision Making, 1666–1736

The last chapter examined the origins of Quakerism and traced its history through the years of early fervor and persecution. The autonomy of the local meeting emerged as central to the peculiarly experiential religion of Friends. What superstructure there was operated irregularly and in strictly advisory relation to the sovereign local meetings. The very existence of such structure was heavily dependent on the need for internal discipline as a rampart against actions like Nayler's, which brought such public opprobrium and persecution on Friends. With the truly harsh governmental action of the early Restoration, this meagre system of gatherings above the local level disintegrated just as a dangerous variant of Naylerism, the teaching of John Perrot, seriously divided the local communities.

This chapter explores the growth of the permanent and effective authority superimposed on local meetings which gradually made local sovereignty more theoretical and less actual. It all began with the drive to combat Perrot's influence.

Solid Structure Above the Local Meetings, 1666–1670

John Perrot died in early September 1665. His movement continued, however, and attracted many; for he had placed personal leadings ahead of group leadings and allowed external conformity with government religious decrees—an easy gospel, indeed. Fox, who had opposed Perrot for some years, was once again in jail. Eleven prominent Friends convened specially in London in May 1666, and approved a strong letter to Friends written by Richard Farnsworth. The burden of their message was that "if any differences arise in the church, . . . we do declare and testify, that the church, with the Spirit of the Lord Jesus Christ, have power, without the assent of such as dissent from their doctrines and practices, to hear and determine the same."[1]

William C. Braithwaite aptly summarizes the impact of this letter: "It obviously marks an important stage in Quaker history. Individual guidance is subordinated to the corporate sense of the Church, which is treated as finding authoritative expression through the elders who are sound in faith. The fellowship is still grounded in a common experience of spiritual life; but agreement with the approved practices and principles which have sprung from that experience is also essential."[2]

Howard Brinton agrees, writing "this letter, by definitely subordinating individual guidance to the sense of the meeting as a whole, marked an important step in Quaker development."[3]

What Braithwaite and Brinton overlook, however, is the drama of the critical situation in which the letter appeared. First, none of the signers of the 1661 disclaimer of violence is numbered among the eleven who wrote this letter. Imprisonment, far-flung travels, and death may account for the absence of the earlier twelve, but the authority of the eleven who spoke in the 1666 letter is unclear.

Admittedly all of the eleven were prominent elders or ministers. But they had no regular authority, being specially convened to write the letter. Furthermore, there were very many equally prominent Quaker ministers and elders to be found in the Perrot camp.[4]

There is no indication of how the elders' letter was received in the months following its publication. What we do know is that George Fox set out immediately upon his release three months after the letter's promulgation to visit as many areas as possible, holding special meetings for reconciliation and establishing monthly business meetings for men and for women wherever these were not functioning. Fox tells us: "But I was so weak with lying about three years in cruel and hard imprisonments, my joints and my body were so stiff and benumbed that I could hardly get on my horse. Neither could I well bend my knee, nor hardly endure fire nor eat warm meat: I had been so long kept from it . . . And though I was very weak, yet I travelled up and down in the service of the Lord."[5]

Why would someone in this condition drag his body through an excruciating journey lasting months? Given the extent of the Perrotonian party, it would appear that Fox believed his movement was in critical danger. He sought reconciliation and introduced a structure that would regularize internal discipline, provide for organizational coordination among local units through quarterly meetings in each region, and capped the operation by establishing a yearly meeting, which was first held at Christmas 1668.[6]

In this four-year period of hectic travel, we have something of a paradox. George Fox kept the movement from falling apart and succeeded in reconciling dissidents by the power of his own clear devotion and his inspired preaching. But what he was "moved of the Lord God"[7] to preach and establish by his charismatic presence was a two-fold institutionalization of charisma. First there was a subordination of all individual leadings to the control of the community, a belief that the Spirit's voice in the gathered community was more reliable than the Spirit's voice within oneself. This made official what had already been standard practice among ministers who regularly tested their leadings by entrusting them to other ministers for "clearance," and to some degree among Friends in general who knew that their actions were under the watchful discernment of the local meeting's overseers. Nor was this action simply a substitution of institution for charisma. It is properly described as substituting communal charismatic decision for individual charismatic decision.

The second form of institutionalization was the establishment of regular quarterly and yearly meetings. True, their procedure was to be according to the same decision rules as the local meetings and their decisions were always advisory. But their very regularity and efficiency soon raised them to a predominant position.

Fox reveals a clear sincerity in the path he chose. He did not make the political atmosphere and the inner strife an opportunity for imposing a structure which would institutionalize his own preeminence. Insofar as he did achieve special status, it came from the extent of his devotion to his communities, a devotion made obvious by his travels in such bad health, and the historical accident that many of the other First Publishers of Truth either died or were permanently imprisoned.[8] Fox's charismatic personal authority comes through clearly in William Penn's generous appreciation:

> And truly, I must say, that though God had visibly clothed him with a *divine preference and authority,* and indeed his very presence expressed a religious majesty, yet he never abused it; but held his place in the Church of God with great meekness and a most engaging humility and modera-

tion. For upon all occasions, like his blessed Master, he was a servant to all; holding and exercising his eldership in the invisible power that had gathered them, with reverence to the Head, and care over the body; and was received only in that spirit and power of Christ, as the first and chief elder in this age; who, as he was therefore worthy of double honour, so for the same reason it was given by the faithful of this day; because his authority was inward and not outward, and that he got it and kept it by the love of God and power of an endless life.

I write by knowledge and not report; and my witness is true, having been with him for weeks and months together on diverse occasions, and those of the nearest and most exercising nature, and that by night and day, by sea and by land, in this and in foreign countries; and I can say I never saw him out of his place, or not a match for every service or occasion.

For in all things he acquitted himself like a man, yea, a strong man, a new and heavenly-minded man, a divine and a naturalist, and all of God Almighty's making.[9]

This is not to say that Fox was faultless nor even that he showed good grace at all times when his personal leadings were not accepted by the community. A telling example of Fox's chagrin at having to subordinate himself to his own institutions appeared a decade later in his 1676 remarks concerning a strongly-worded polemic which the "Second-day's* Morning Meeting" of men ministers had refused to let him circulate: Fox wrote, "I was not moved to set up that meeting to make orders against the reading of my papers."[10] By 1676, Fox's charisma, too, was under institutional control.

With Fox's hectic journeys from 1666 to 1670, then, we get the initiation of a firm system of governance. And, because of Fox's successful campaign, the letter of 1666 from the eleven elders became the procedure for resolving future conflicts between individual community leadings.

Individual Discernment and Personal Infallibility

In order to understand a bit more clearly the leadings we have been discussing, we might take a few pages here to explore the concept of spiritual discernment. Spiritual discernment is the ability to differentiate reliable leadings from unreliable ones.

George Fox tells us that he received two separate gifts early in his spiritual life. First, "the spiritual discerning came into me, by which I did discern my own thoughts, groans and sighs, and what it was that did veil me, and what it was that did open me." Subsequently, he received a gift

* Monday

22

of discerning others' spirits "through which I saw plainly that when many people talked of God, the Serpent spoke in them. And a report went abroad of me that I was a young man that had a discerning spirit."[11] These two gifts are examples of charisma in the New Testament sense—intense gratuitous presence in an individual of a quality which builds up the Christian community.[12]

Fox's power of discernment, his reading of the Inner Light, was the root of his apostolic decision making. He believed his discernment to be incapable of error, that it was infallible. "I was commanded to turn people to that inward light, spirit and grace . . . which I infallibly knew would never deceive any."[13] Fox's claim of infallible knowledge was consistent with his antecedents. The Seekers, for example, believed that in the Apostolic Age "all was administered under the anointing of the Spirit, clearly, certainly, infallibly." Not so in this age of apostasy. Therefore, "they waited for an Apostle, or some one with a visible glory and power, able in the Spirit to give visible demonstration of being sent."[14] And, for many, Fox was just such a man.

Nor was the belief limited to Fox. Edward Burrough, one of the chief Publishers of Truth wrote, "The judgment in that matter [heresy] must be just, equal, Holy and [only] by the Spirit of Christ, which is infallible, and gives infallibility of judgment and discerning into all cases and things."[15]

Quaker belief in infallible inspiration by the Spirit drew barbs from adversaries. These critics attempted to pinpoint weak arguments in Quaker tracts, arguing that any such error proved that Quaker leadings were not divinely inspired. One such critic concluded his 1674 argument that "your Books must be false; and consequently not the issue of the infallible Spirit, as you would have the world believe they are."[16]

Modern apologists for the Society of Friends have occasionally attempted to minimize this dimension of Quaker origins. Henry Van Etten, for example, asserts, "It must be remembered that he [George Fox] did not use the word 'Truth' in any exclusive sense, and that he never believed himself infallible."[17] In reality, Fox considered infallible knowledge of God's will to be so universal a gift that it even appears in a 1663 tract on marriage which he coauthored with Thomas Lawrence. When asked "whether freedom from all sin, and infallible assurance of God's will be of absolute necessity" for marriage, he replied, "To have infallible assurance [that] there is freedom from all sin, to hunger and thirst, and press after it, to witness a growth, to be sincere in heart, and faith to God in measure, is of absolute necessity."[18]

Fox's own reliance on inspiration was so complete that it led him far beyond the strictly religious realm. We have noted above his brief flirtation with the practice of medicine as the result of an enlightenment about the inner nature of creatures. William Braithwaite suggests that similar inspiration lay behind Fox's attempt to demonstrate the correctness of using "thou" for one person and "you" for many. "He seems in some way to have regarded himself as possessing a spiritual counterpart to human learning, which took him above and beyond it.[19]

The same conviction that his inspiration was infallible led Fox, long after the event, to rationalize his behaviour in Lichfield in a manner which Christopher Hill considers "singularly unconvincing."[20]

More generally, writes Braithwaite, this belief in infallible inspiration led to a "forcefulness and also [a] mixture of unperceived error [in early Quaker apologists], e.g., confident preaching in the face of persecution but also intolerance, deprecation of the value of intellectual gifts, frequent extravagance of conduct. The violent language often used showed a want of charity, which was only to be excused because the Quaker was convinced that he was infallibly right."[21]

It was Nayler's fall that first cast serious doubt on personal infallibility. Here, indeed, was a pillar of the church who was so clearly deceived as to bring ridicule on Friends. Yet what controls could be introduced to test inspiration without denying inspiration altogether?[22]

Tests of Leadings: The Cross

The earliest major test of one's leading seems to have been whether one finds the Cross in what he is drawn to. Wrote Fox, "To speak of truth when ye are moved, it is a cross to the will; if ye live in the truth which ye speak, ye live in the cross of your own wills."[23] So, too, Richard Farnsworth wrote in 1652 that "you will be brought into a discerning, to savour truth from error, both in yourselves, and also in one another" if you will follow the cross which will "cross and crucify that which would consult with human wisdom and reason." And thus, "that which is earthly, carnal, and brutish, will be cut down in you."

Ten days later, Farnsworth exhorted the newly convinced* Margaret Fell to "keep in the cross, and purity will grow;—the safest way is in the cross: take up the cross daily; mind to be guided by that which crosseth your own wills, and it will bring every idle word, thought and deed to

* Converted

24

judgment in you; and so the old man will be crucified, with the affections and lusts thereof."[24]

The appropriateness of this test of one's leadings is especially clear if one recalls that Quakers needed to dissociate themselves from the licentious Ranters who "fled the cross." Actions from the true Spirit were therefore seen by Friends as always contrary to self-will.[25]

But as a positive mark of divine leadings, the presence of the cross left much to be desired. Friends found themselves justifying many unwise actions "partly because of the strong call under which they were exercised, but mainly because they were contrary to Friends' natural inclination and so involved a very real taking of the cross."[26]

Thus, the practice of going naked as a sign—a display last seen among the Munster Anabaptists—was not disowned by Quaker leaders. James Nayler, in 1654, says that the Friends who acted this way acted contrary to their own will.[27] Vernon Noble tells us of the reception of this sort of witness at Oxford.

> These two young girls from Kendal . . . went the wrong way about converting the riotous university scholars and they were soundly beaten for it. Elizabeth Fletcher, a dainty girl of 17, took off all her clothes and walked through the streets "contrary to her own will or inclination, in obedience to the Lord." She was described as "a very modest, grave young woman," and this startling behavior was to be a sign that God would strip the people of their hypocrisy.[28]

As late as 1672, the intellectual author of the *Apology*, Robert Barclay, called the city of Aberdeen to repentance by walking three of the main streets in sack cloth and ashes. The criterion of action: he did not want to do it.[29]

Tests of Leadings: Scripture

Although one might expect that Scripture would be of help in sorting out some of the leadings of early Friends, there is not much satisfying evidence. For example, those who went naked at Munster noted the biblical passage of the prophet Isaiah who went naked for six months as a testimony to the doom of Jerusalem.[30] Other scriptural passages could be cited which urged modesty or avoidance of scandal,[31] but who was to say which scriptural strand was more appropriate.

As J. William Frost comments, the Friends, like all other Christian communities, had their own special emphases in reading Scripture. They heard literally Matthew's injunction to "swear not at all." But, "although they

25

believed in the duty of charity, they did not echo Christ's advice to the rich young ruler to 'sell all that thou hast, and distribute unto the poor.' " Again:

> Friends refused to bow; when opponents mentioned that Abraham bowed to the children of Heth and Lot to the two angels, Barclay argued that the practice of the patriarchs was not to be the practice of today or else polygamy would be allowed. Yet, since the Old Testament was much clearer than the New Testament about forbidding mixed marriages, Friends used as a precedent the passages in Genesis where the giants became sinful because they married daughters of the earth and Jacob pleased his parents by marrying one of Isaac's kin while Esau displeased them by marrying a Hittite.[32]

In a sense, the problem Quakers faced was even more fundamental. Other Protestant communities, no matter how they decided what Scripture meant, held that Scripture itself was normative. For Fox, his comrades, and successors, only the Spirit of God—the Inner Light—was normative. The Holy Spirit, not Scripture, was the "touchstone and judge by which . . . to try all doctrines, religions, and opinions and to end all controversies." Fox noted that he reached his own early leadings entirely by the inspiration of the Spirit, not from Scripture. Only subsequently did he turn to Scripture, always finding, of course, that it was possible to construe its meaning according to his enlightenment. In this sense, he remarked, "Yet I had no slight esteem of the Holy Scriptures, and what the Lord opened to me I afterward found was agreeable to them."[33] Nor was Fox ready to limit this power of understanding to himself. In 1658 he wrote: "That which may be known of God is manifest within people. Thou needest no man to teach thee."[34]

Friends found themselves in a permanently ambiguous situation. Robert Barclay, for example, could explain that "because the Spirit of God is the Fountain of all Truth and sound reason, therefore, we have well said, That *it cannot contradict neither the Testimony of the Scripture, nor right reason.*"[35] The Inner Light or the Spirit, however, provided the test of the meaning of Scripture and of the rightness of reason.

We are not saying that Friends threw out Scripture. In fact, when some of the extreme followers of John Perrot did so, perhaps even burning their Bibles, they were castigated for it by Fox's party. Clearly, however, the authority of Scripture remained secondary to an individual's strong inner leadings.[36]

Tests of Leadings: Submission of Openings

It is no surprise that early preachers found it expedient to submit their leadings to each other as a way of testing or letting the "self-consistence of the Spirit" become operative. For instance, in 1659, Aldam wrote Fox and Burrough to "take into your consideration the things written downe in that power which came to mee and W. Dewsbury at Yorke and lett mee have an answer, how the Large wisdom of God in you doth aprove of the particular thinges to bee done, and what it disaproves of, that in one Mynde wee may meete."[37]

The same attitude appears in the informal First Day meetings of London ministers who would gather to share ideas before dispersing to preach at the different meetings in the area.

Tests of Leadings: The Fruits of the Holy Spirit

But, when Friends gathered, be they ministers on First Day or all the brethren in local meeting for business, how were they to know whose leading was genuine and whose was not? The early literature abounds in descriptions of the fruits of the good and evil spirits. The principle of God within, writes Fox, produced soberness, peace, stillness, quietness, and strength. The transgression of the principle of God resulted in distractions, distempers, unruliness, and confusion. Another epistle listed the fruits of the good spirit as "tender love, unity, grace, and good order" as well as "a sweetness and harmony of life, unity, and subjection to one another, and a preserving one another in the Lord." In essence the assorted lists turn out to be variants of the Pauline catalogue of fruits of the Holy Spirit: "love, joy, peace, patience, kindness, goodness, faithfulness, gentleness, self-control." The litany boiled down to the "presence of inner peace" which Howard Brinton characterizes as "the main Quaker test of right guidance." As Barclay put it, "And since there is no greater Mark of the People of God, than to be at Peace among themselves; whatsoever tendeth to break that Bond of Love and Peace, must be testified against."[38]

Later Tests of Leadings: Silence, Unadorned Speech

With the passage of time, the community drew upon its experience to add some supplemental tests of reliable leadings. Barclay underscored the importance of the silence in a meeting; internal silence was necessary if one was to "discern . . . *the still, small Voice* of the Spirit." One who was waiting for the Lord in inner silence could not be deceived because "the *Excellency* of this *silent waiting upon God* doth appear, in that it is impossible for the *Enemy,* viz, the *Devil,* to counterfeit it, so as for any Soul to be deceived or deluded by him in the Exercise thereof."[39]

27

Additionally, a special plain style of speech in meeting was taken as a sign of genuine inspiration. Penn described Fox as such a speaker.

> And abruptly and brokenly as sometimes his sentences would fall from him about divine things, it is well known they were often as tests to many fairer declarations. And indeed it showed, beyond all contradiction, that God sent him, that no arts or parts had any share in his matter or manner of his ministry; and that so many great, excellent, and necessary truths as he came forth to preach to mankind had therefore nothing of man's wit or wisdom to recommend them.[40]

Limitations of Friends Tests of Leadings

Friends tests were not fully reliable. Simplicity of speech could always be fabricated by those who knew that an audience favored such a style. Inner silence could be fabricated, too, so that even the individual who sought to be silent might be deceived. And harmony of the group could be achieved by excluding those who disagreed—the history of Quaker schisms shows how readily a divided community can split into separate camps each of which manifests *internal* love and unity.

More basically, the Friends doctrine of discernment lacked a number of the assets of other religious traditions. First, belief in corruption of nature led Friends to replace reason solely with direct inspiration. In an insightful paragraph, J. William Frost explains, "Both Friends and Puritans recognized the necessity of something other than reason in religion, but with this difference: The Puritans used and defended all possible tools of man in learning about and communicating the contents of revelation; the Friends admitted only supernatural means in evaluating supernatural matters."[41]

Secondly, Friends lacked—at least at the beginning—a theological tradition. Surrounded with a sampler of theological positions on every possible topic, early Quakers constantly used the Spirit to discern which of these theologies was correct. Many issues such as war or pacifism, marriage with or without officiating witnesses, independent local units or one of the many variants of central control or some combination of the two— these were areas that had to be determined *before* Friends had developed a distinctive tradition which they could then use as a criterion for judging the merits of each fresh concern. We shall see how quickly Friends created and sanctified such a tradition—a mark in itself of how badly some sort of objective test was needed.

Finally, strictly in the area of assessing the person's inner motions, Friends clearly seem to have been deprived of a working knowledge of the literature of discernment that had preceded them. While there were precedents for Quaker belief in guidance by the Holy Spirit (see Appendix A), a reading of the letters of Fox and early Friends does not reveal that this general inclination to trust the Spirit was accompanied by an understanding of the nuances of discernment as it had developed and flourished from the Fathers of the Desert to the mystic who founded the Jesuits, Ignatius of Loyola (1491–1556).[42]

For example, Loyola's approach made a basic distinction among leadings. There was a special kind of spiritual experience that was "without any previous cause through which a soul might be led to such a consolation through its own acts of intellect and will." This "experience of transcendence" was reliable and self-authenticating to the person who experienced it. All other inward experiences could come from either the good or the evil spirit. The whole question of infallibility which plagued Friends was thus eliminated by Ignatius. Certainty was attached only to the rare special sorts of visitations of the first category, and even these visitations could be tested by outsiders. Ignatius could rely on the objective goodness and badness of actions which could be determined by natural law as well as on the rich tradition and legislation of the Roman Church because "it is necessary that all matters of which we wish to make a choice be either indifferent or good in themselves, and such that they are lawful within our Holy Mother, the hierarchical Church, and not bad or opposed to her."

Loyola proceeded to suggest guidelines for discovering the hidden meanings of the inner leadings which were not in the special self-authenticating class. After much weighing of inner experiences, individual decisions could be made by heading in the direction where genuine peace seemed most to lie, but the decision was never made with certainty.[43]

What was true in individual discernment was equally so in the case of a group. Loyola's earliest companions gathered with him to discern God's will for them. Although they sought to find the Spirit and achieve unity in their conclusions ("todos contentos"), they made no claim of infallibility in their attempt.[44]

For Fox, there was no adequate distinction between types of spiritual leadings and no external yardstick by which to measure such individual leadings. No wonder the meeting came to assume so central a role. For only the inspired group was available to act as a check on the individual's inspiration.

We have already seen how this reliance on the meeting's unity officially triumphed over individual inspiration in the ministers' letter of 1666. Now

29

we shall see how the local meetings themselves gradually became subject to the unifying influence of the higher levels of meetings which slowly ate away at local autonomy.

Defeat of Localism: The Wilkinson-Story Dispute: 1670–1676

Let us return to the development of Quaker structures. In the 1660–1670 period, Fox was busy establishing regular monthly, quarterly, and yearly meetings, with the first yearly meeting held in 1668. This newly created system had two results. First, there was a "bracing effect upon the Society" giving "the strength that comes from a well devised organization." But there was a drawback as well because "the natural result was not merely to coordinate the discernment of the community with the spiritual leadings of the individual, but to enlarge continuously, by the successive encroachments with which a system of organization aggrandizes itself, the area of conduct over which the community exerted absolute sway."[45]

Eventually, the community's sway would touch even the cut of one's clothes. If such excess was not experienced immediately, the potential was clearly there and recognized. An anonymous 1673 pamphlet railed against the "Foxonian-unity" which stigmatized those Friends who dissented from a decision because they were not inwardly moved to favor it as being God's truth. The result was "to deprive us of the law of the Spirit and to bring in a tyrannical government: it would lead us from the rule within to subject us to a rule without."

The anti-Fox pamphlet also cited supposed abuses from outside the local meetings. There was too much rooting out of error, too much external programming of supposedly spontaneous meetings for worship in order to assure that the recognized ministers monopolized the time with their preaching, thus eliminating both the time of silence and the chance for ordinary members of the community to minister [preach] if they felt so moved.[46]

Fox was on a missionary journey to America at the time, so the abuses—to the extent that they were real—were laid at his door because of the system he had established rather than because of his personal actions. The pamphlet proved unsuccessful in some quarters because Friends were still so painfully aware of the perils of disunity which Perrot's similar views had caused, and as one might expect, the pamphlet was rebutted by the 1673 Yearly Meeting.

By 1675, however, with Fox back in England, a group which had endorsed the 1673 pamphlet formed around two traditionalist leaders, John

Wilkinson and John Story. This duo called for a return to the individual freedom and local autonomy which had been prevalent prior to 1666. In addition, their affirmation that one need not provoke persecution from the government was ambiguously close in expression to Perrot's argument that one need not accept persecution at all,[47] a phenomenon making them at once liable to accusation from Fox's group and attractive to many who had followed Perrot.

Finally, in 1676, the ministers gathered for their yearly meeting and affirmed that "the Power of God is the authority of the men's and women's meetings and of all the other meetings."[48] Individual Friends' leadings, when they contradicted the decision of the meeting, were not to be followed. The authority of local meetings was not attacked, of course, and superior meetings remained only advisory. But there was no attempt to force these new units to refrain from issuing definitive "advice." The Wilkinson-Story party went into schism.

An example of this forceful "advice" was the decision of the Yearly Meeting of Ministers in the following year. Now happily unified because it was free of the unrepresented Wilkinson-Story faction, the meeting felt drawn to "reprove and judge that jealous, rending and separating spirit (of Wilkinson and Story). By that salt which we have in ourselves from the Lord are we enabled to savor between the transformation of the enemy and the scruples of the innocent, and, as to be tender to the one, so to give judgment against the other."[49]

Officially, of course, nothing had changed. The 1676 Yearly Meeting of Ministers had been careful to avow that "all the faithful men and women in every county, city, and nation, whose faith stands in the power of God, have all right to the power of the meeting, for they be the heirs of the Power and Authority."[50]

In 1678, elders representing the country districts met for a yearly meeting and received a gracious letter from the ministers' yearly meeting declaring that the latter utterly rejected "all power, authority and government in the Church of Christ that is not exercised in the holy power and free spirit of the Lord."[51]

Robert Barclay and *The Anarchy of the Ranters*, 1674

As one can readily understand, the victory of corporate over individual discernment carried its own difficulties. Friends started with the primitive conviction that the Spirit infallibly guided them. But, when harsh experience showed that sometimes the individual could err, people tended to decide that the community which judged their leadings should assume the infallibility which they had previously attributed to themselves. The next step—in a period when units above the local meetings were still emerging—was to argue that local meetings were not the ultimate focus of infallibility, but the yearly (national) meeting was.

Robert Barclay, a young Scotsman of twenty-eight who had been a Friend for only six years, addressed this problem in his 1674 booklet, *The Anarchy of the Ranters,* a carefully thought-out defense of Fox's new form of ecclesiastical polity. Although the book was an effective weapon against the Wilkinson-Story party, Barclay later commented that he knew nothing of this group at the time he wrote.[52] Barclay first sought to eliminate infallibility as a necessary adjunct of either individual or group decisions. Then he set out constructing a new basis for church government.

Recent authors show a penchant for misreading Barclay. Arnold Lloyd, for example, asserts that in *The Anarchy of the Ranters,* Barclay upheld the "infallible Voice of the Spirit in the doctrinal positions held in common by Church leaders." Lloyd accuses him of an "emphasis on infallibility quite out of harmony with the Seeker temper" of the original Quakers.[53] The opposite was quite true.

Barclay wished to steer a middle course between those who put infallibility in every individual leading and those who made every action of the gathered meeting infallible. This task was not easy because some form of infallibility was held by every Christian church. He argued that Matthew 18 did guarantee that the "Gates of Hell shall not prevail" against the church and therefore that it must be truly guided by the Spirit in crisis situations. But infallibility was the property of the Spirit, not of men. Barclay wrote that "the only proper Judge of Controversies in the Church, is the Spirit of God, and the Power of deciding solely lies in it; as having the only unerring, infallible and certain Judgment belonging to it; which infallibility is not necessarily annexed to any Persons, Person or Places whatsoever, by Virtue of any Office, Place or Station any one may have or have had in the Body of Christ."[54]

Furthermore, an individual or group judgment was infallible only if it fully expressed the Spirit's leading: "The Judgment of a certain Person or Persons in certain cases is infallible, not because they are infallible, but because in these Things, and at that Time they were led by the infallible Spirit."

Hence, Quaker infallibility differed from the Protestant version which was present whenever there was a "Synod or Council" representing all true Churches of Christ. And Friends certainly differed from Papists who held that infallibility occured if there was "Plurality of the Votes" and agreement by "the Pope and his Legates." For Friends, in the event of a crisis so serious that the "Gates of Hell" threaten to prevail, "there will be an *infallible Judgment* from the Spirit of God, which may be in a General Assembly; yet not limited to it, as excluding others: And may prove to be the Judgment of the *Plurality;* yet not to be decided thereby, as if the *Infallibility* were placed there, excluding the fewer." In brief, therefore, the *"Infallible Judgment* from the Spirit of God" would inevitably occur, but "either in one or other, few or more."

For Barclay, then, infallibility was a mark of the church in time of crisis. But infallibility was not fixed in any body or individual. Instead, it was found in the person or group which most clearly manifested the signs of the Spirit's presence. Barclay's infallibility, therefore, was reduced to an unobtrusive minimum. It was only guaranteed to appear in a radical crisis of the church, but in no predetermined place. Its presence would be discerned by the faithful, whether the utterance was from a yearly meeting of ministers or an otherwise undistinguished member of a local meeting. Barclay definitively freed Quakerism from the taunts of such contemporary critics as William Allen who accused Friends of "pretending to as much infallibility in *your Body* representative in managing it, as the Papists do in reference to the Pope."[55]

Having eliminated infallibility as the source of authority of the various meetings, Barclay justified the exercise of governmental authority on more traditional ecclesiastical lines. Ordinarily, he told us, those who had the higher spiritual gifts, the ministers and elders, were specially blessed with the Spirit's guidance, but not inevitably. For the church's good order, these people of known ability to discern were to be encouraged by other members of the church to "instruct, reprove, yea, and command in some cases."[56]

Thus, the basis for decision making was effectively changed. Friends had always had great respect for the opinions of such weighty members as the travelling ministers. But now, with the local communities' decisions no longer infallibly guaranteed by the gathered unity in which the decision was reached, authority was prudently attributed by Friends to the gatherings which were blessed with the presence of the largest number of ministers and elders. Quarterly and especially yearly meeting decisions thus afforded far more respect than those of the local meeting.

Having thus established the authority of the new superstructure,

Barclay went on to establish the limited but real power of church government. The needs of the community required the conformity of its members when the issue involved "fundamental Principles and Doctrines of Faith," and even in some secondary matters (Barclay referred to the circumcision controversy in Acts 15), there was to be unity without such uniformity that individual gifts and needs were slighted.[57] Although the forms of government Fox had set up and which Barclay justified were not really as sensitive to individual gifts as Barclay hoped, Barclay succeeded in giving a presumption of correctness to the decisions of the community, especially to the decisions of the ministers gathered in yearly meeting, but without claiming infallibility for them. No longer did the individual Friend obey a decision because he or she had participated in the decision making process and had felt the presence of the Spirit. Instead, individuals accepted the decision on faith that the elders and ministers, gathered in a meeting he or she did not attend, had been spiritually led to this decision.

In the past, advisories from such nonlocal gatherings got their power from the local meeting's religious experience at the time it considered them. This is why Fox's presence in each local meeting, not the authority of the writers, was needed to gain acceptance for the 1666 ministers' letter against Perrot's group. Now, though local meetings would still go through the form of accepting the "advice" of the yearly meeting, Barclay had succeeded in transferring the real authority to the presumed spiritual insight of the remote regional or national assembly.

Barclay's desire to protect Friends against meetings claiming the automatic infallibility which Friends had previously claimed for themselves as individuals was certainly prescient. Already in 1680, a group of eighty-two Friends in Barbados—where Perrotism and the Wilkinson-Story movements had both been very active—attempted to escape some of the excess individualism within these two groups by swinging too far the other way. They subscribed to the following statement:

> I desire to give up my whole concern, if required, both spiritual and temporal, unto the judgment of the Spirit of God in the Men and Women's Meetings, as believing it to be more according to the universal wisdom of God than any particular measure, in myself or any particulars [i.e., individuals], with which the Men and Women's Meetings have not unity.[58]

Fox and two other notables, George Whitehead and Alexander Parker, wrote to request that the statement be dropped since it overstated the role of the meeting and would be a ball for the Wilkinson-Story cannon.

The movement to accentuate the authority of the meeting finally reached its extreme expression in George Keith, a noted Quaker intellectual and polemicist. His explicit claim that "all decisions of meetings for discipline should be regarded as infallibly determined by the Holy Spirit" led to confrontation and, finally, expulsion (disownment) by the yearly meeting in 1695.[59]

Robert Barclay and the *Apology*, 1676

Barclay's skill as a polemecist quickly made him emerge as a prime spokesman for the pro-Fox group during the Wilkinson-Story dispute. At the conclusion of that struggle, Barclay issued his master work, the *Apology.* This extensive justification of Quaker belief was eloquently enunciated in the combination of Cartesian and scholastic language then in vogue. Widely accepted by Friends from the very beginning, the *Apology* became a mainstay not only of external polemics but, more importantly, of Quaker self-understanding.[60]

Because the *Apology* was so widely consulted by Friends, one should not be overly surprised to see it blamed for the rigidities which became apparent in Quakerism in the years after its publication. Rufus M. Jones was particularly strong in this judgment at the turn of the present century. Jones' own reputation among Friends has been so hallowed that his assessment of Barclay has received less challenge than it deserves.

Jones tells us that Quakerism shifted from the "dynamic affirmation mysticism of the first period (1648–1676) to a passive and negative type"—the quietism of eighteenth century Quakerism—because of Barclay's theology in which "every spiritual action is miraculous." Thus, man initiates nothing, he merely waits for God to act.[61]

Barclay, according to Jones, tied Friends' "fresh discovery of spiritual truth" to the "ancient dogmatic theory of 'man.' " Rufus Jones writes further that "what I regret most is that the early formulation of Quakerism should have been made as an adjustment with the Augustinian and Calvinistic system instead of following the fresh and transforming path which the spiritual reformers, the real forerunners and progenitors of 'the Children of the Light' had discovered."

At the root of Barclay's error, charges Jones, is his acceptance of the Calvinist doctrine of original sin and corrupt human nature. Jones becomes somewhat emotional in his appeal to personal experience: "No attempt is made to sound the deeps of human experience itself. It does not occur to [Barclay] that this is a question to be settled by the testimony of the soul, and that first of all one ought to investigate actual human life as it is and to build the theory on facts of experience."[62]

Building from this base, Jones goes on to contend that Barclay's quietism, like all quietism, gives no criteria for distinguishing true from false lights because the gap between supposedly corrupt nature and divine grace makes it impossible for the "higher" spiritual movements to be tested by the "lower" activity of human reason. For Barclay, there was no test, no criterion of true leadings. For Jones, inner experience of the divine is natural, not supernatural. Reason can therefore be the test.[63]

Jones' line of argument is by no means without its followers. This writer has often encountered it when interviewing contemporary Friends. Such an estimable authority as Arnold Lloyd adopted it in 1950: "[Barclay's] theory of the divine in man cannot be reconciled with the original Quaker message. It was widely read and was a considerable factor in the decline into quietism in the eighteenth century. [Barclay] regarded the divine and the human as mutually exclusive categories."[64]

It is true, of course, that Barclay held a very "Protestant" view of the degeneracy of man: "*All* Adam's *Posterity* . . . is fallen, degenerated, and dead." Unlike the Calvinists, however, Barclay argued that the Inner Light or Divine Seed was a supernatural gift to *every* man which opened to each the chance to achieve perfection. On the other hand, Barclay did indeed argue that a Quaker should wait for the Lord's initiative in worship and decisions about action instead of simply relying upon his spontaneous inclination.[65]

But in these arguments Barclay was not creating a new theory but expressing traditional Quaker belief. In 1654, Francis Howgill and Edward Burrough—outstanding among the earliest of the First Publishers—wrote to Margaret Fell that they had argued against the magistrates of Bristol who "said the light was natural and that every one had it not."[66] Had not Fox declared in 1663 that the true Christian must necessarily "wait on God, in his Light to receive his counsel; [for] how else do Friends differ from the World?"[67]

Even Isaac Penington, an early Friend whose name is often associated with those opposing the new structures of government, is guilty of the basic distinction between natural and supernatural orders which underlies the preceding quotations. William Braithwaite, after lauding Penington, concludes that "he was fettered by the dualistic thought of the age, which put the natural and the Divine in two separate compartments, and accordingly he fails, like others of the early Friends, to reach a unified conception either of human personality or of the person of Christ."[68]

In short, if Fox and his earliest brethren believed that the saving action of Christ could raise them back to the "state of Adam before he fell," a fortiori they held that there was need of such elevation. Therefore, Fox's man was by nature a sinner.[69]

It seems safe to conclude, then, that Barclay was not the source of the cleavage between natural and supernatural in man nor of the passive quietism that called Quakers to wait for the Lord's initiatives. Barclay was simply a faithful and clear expositor of the great bulk of what beliefs Friends already held. Dean Freiday, editor of the most recent edition of the *Apology*, criticizes Barclay for underplaying the "confessional and practical significance (so important for Fox) [of Christ] the Cornerstone." But Freiday also emphasizes that the "Quaker doctrine of the supernatural Inward Light of Christ" is "beautifully developed by Barclay" in a "systematic presentation of what Fox was trying to say."[70]

In a limited sense, of course, there is truth in Jones' allegation. Barclay wrote clearly and authoritatively, and was republished by Quaker leaders with enthusiasm. For the first time, Friends had a source book to which they could turn when in doubt about what Fox and his early followers had taught. This meant that Fox's thought suddenly became more effective in unifying Quaker practice simply because it was suddenly so readily available. Fox's skepticism about human reason and his quietism in the face of human dilemmas were now expressed in Barclay's clear language for every Friend to ponder. In short, Barclay did not present a doctrine which could not "be reconciled with the original Quaker message."[71] Barclay presented, in clear and distinct terms, that very message. The one thing in Barclay's writings not found in the earliest Quaker sources is his justification of the new governing structures which Fox had done so much to establish. Insofar as these new structures would eventually weaken the life of the local meetings, Barclay can be criticized; but even here he shares the blame with Fox.

The British myth that the king can do no wrong has led Englishmen to blame the royal advisors for regal blunders. So, too, Catholics have wagged their tongues about the evil men of the Roman Curia who were supposedly "holding back" information from the ever-benevolent Pope. Perhaps, Rufus Jones was guilty of a similar fallacy when he attacked Barclay for creating detrimental doctrines that in fact originated with George Fox. If Barclay sinned, it could only have been in saying clearly in one tract what Fox had put forward in an unsystematic variety of utterances.

The Gradual Ascendance of Central Hegemony, 1676–1736

With the successful exclusion of the lack of structure proposed by Wilkinson and Story, the rise of central predominance was only a matter of time. Let us quickly sketch the way the development occurred.

The Meeting for Sufferings as Lobby and Legal Aid Society

The key to Quaker government became the Meeting for Sufferings, established by the Yearly Meeting of 1675 to act on its behalf when it was not in session. As the name implies, the Meeting for Sufferings had as its first duty the alleviation of misery for those Friends who were feeling the heavy sting of persecution. The body met weekly from 1676 onwards "that the cruelty and opressions (which also under pretence of Law are committed) tending to the ruine of Innocent families may not be hid *but be laid before those in power to redress time.*"[72] At its first meeting, in October 1675, the Meeting for Sufferings quickly agreed "that Friends' sufferings be layd upon those in power" and appointed a subcommittee to "draw up some instances of most gross sufferings to be presented to the Parliament."[73]

The whole network of quarterly meetings was marshaled to achieve a change in the Recusancy Laws so that Friends might not suffer so cruelly. Each quarter (county quarterly meeting) appointed one Friend to come up to London at the beginning of parliamentary sessions to lobby the local member of parliament under the coordinating guidance of the Meeting for Sufferings. In 1676, arrangement was made for regular correspondence between the Meeting for Sufferings and each quarterly meeting. From this base an effective series of letters, personal presentations and printed propaganda was put together, and Quakers were deprived of changes in the law in 1679 and 1681 only because of untimely royal dissolutions of parliamentary sessions. By 1679, the Meeting for Sufferings was using its county network to organize the Quaker vote in an effort to ensure the return of those members of parliament who favored Friends.

The period from 1681 to 1688 saw a temporary end to Friends' parliamentary lobbying for the simple reason that Parliament was for the most part out of session. A smooth switch of tactics led the Meeting for Sufferings to private interventions with influential judges, bishops, ex-members of parliament, and peers as persecution continued on an even harsher basis than while Parliament was in session.

After the Glorious Revolution of 1688–1689 installed William and Mary, the Toleration Act gave basic freedom of public worship to Friends.

However, the new religious toleration made no provision for many Friends' practices, including their objections to taking oaths and paying tithes. The Meeting for Sufferings returned to its previous pattern of political lobbying, although on a more intense and coordinated pattern. At the same time, it found itself relaying to the quarterly and monthly meetings not only all the latest actions of Parliament touching Friends, but also the successful strategies used to defend Friends in court. So complete was the coordination that N.C. Hunt remarks, "In this respect the Meeting for Sufferings, linked as it was with the country-wide Quaker network, was obviously ensuring by action in the Courts that the law as enacted by Parliament was being applied correctly in regard to detail throughout the length and breadth of the country."[74]

The Meeting for Sufferings continued its campaigns on behalf of Friends. Because it was on the scene in London, its advice came to be obeyed without challenge by the less well-informed quarterly and monthly meetings. Hunt goes on to describe in detail the four major campaigns between 1696 and 1736 which were conducted by the Meeting for Sufferings to repeal those laws which restricted Friends.[75] The growth of the authority of the Meeting for Sufferings was in large measure a natural outgrowth of the need for centralized coordination if the campaigns to influence legislation were to succeed.

The Affirmation Act of 1696 allowed Friends to "declare in the presence of Almighty God" instead of swearing. But some Friends found this still too much like an oath to satisfy their reading of the Matthean injunction to "swear not at all."[76] The Yearly Meeting of 1702 allowed those who were dissatisfied with the wording to organize their own campaign for new legislation. Their efforts, not abetted by the Meeting for Sufferings, produced only successive failures which culminated in 1712 when the unofficial campaign to reword the affirmation ran counter to efforts by the Meeting for Sufferings to obtain renewal of the about-to-expire 1696 Act. The divided loyalty of members of parliament who were sympathetic to friends spelled defeat for both campaigns. In 1715, the next occasion for seeking parliamentary action, the Meeting for Sufferings co-opted the unofficial campaigners. First, it promised to make "sincere endeavours" to get a wording acceptable to the unhappy Friends. If that proved impossible, they promised to take care that "the present affirmation not be lost."[77]

The sincere endeavours turned out to be an unenthusiastic presentation of new wording which was rejected by the Commons on the same day it was proposed. The token attempt now complete, the serious campaign which had been shrewdly pushed all along moved into high gear. The original Affirmation Act of 1696 quickly was elevated to a permanent place in the Statute Book. In the process, the Meeting for Sufferings moved subtly into the position of becoming the Society of Friends' sole contact with Parliament.[78]

The extent of the Meeting for Sufferings' growing hegemony in this area is illustrated by a 1735 incident. In that year, York Quarterly Meeting decided to write some members of parliament asking for a tithe bill to include a clause enabling Quakers to serve as sheriffs, aldermen, and jurors. The Meeting for Sufferings was aghast by the action since it had its own strategy which called for no such additions to the bill. It arranged to admonish the York Friends for "this independent and irresponsible action."[79]

The point is not that the Meeting for Sufferings was being unreasonable or usurping power. However, if it was to lobby effectively for Friends, it had to assume central supervision of all Quaker action which could affect the attitudes of members of parliament. But there was no avoiding the basic tension this central power created. Gradually, bit by bit, the local meetings lost their sovereignty. Quakerism was saved from further persecution by a central institution whose very existence was in conflict with the founding Quaker principle that decisions were based on local experience in common with God's leadings.

The Meeting for Sufferings as Arbiter of the Externals of Life

It would be naive, perhaps, to think that structure so effective in marshaling Friends' political life could be limited to political endeavors alone. After all, the success of Friends in influencing Parliament depended on their reputation throughout the country. Anything that could damage that reputation was therefore appropriate matter for central concern. All externals soon become grist for the central mill. William Braithwaite observed that "the new instrument of Church government was a ready means for retrenching extravagances which gave insidious entrance to the spirit of the world; and zealous Friends did not see that they were substituting legalism for liberty, the control of the form for the control of the Spirit.[80]

Before long, Quakers—even as they entered the economic middle class—took on the separateness of dress and life-style that would characterize them well into the nineteenth century. Already in 1700, George Fox's widow, Margaret Fell, would write an epistle of pained exasperation as she watched Friends transformed.

> For it is now gone forty-seven years since we owned the Truth, and all
> things has gone well till now of late that this narrowness and strictness
> is entering in, that cannot tell what to do or not do. Our Monthly and
> Quarterly Meetings were set up for reproving and looking into suspicious
> and disorderly walking . . . and not [for] private persons to take upon
> them to make order and say, This must be done and the other must be
> done. Christ Jesus saith, That we must take no thought what we shall
> eat or what we shall drink but bids us consider the lilies, howe they grow
> in more royalty than Solomon. But contrary to this, we must not look
> at no colours, nor make anything that is changeable colours, as the hills
> are, nor sell them, nor wear them. But we must be all in one dress and
> one colour. This is a silly poor gospel.[81]

But Margaret Fell's warning went unheeded. Friends won political
liberty at the price of personal and local religious autonomy. The
personally-felt leadings of the Spirit, whether experienced in private or
in the local meeting, were supplemented and, to a large extent, supplanted
by the directions received from higher structural entities.

Of interest to the general study of organizations is the curious way
in which Quaker experience in the period we have traced both confirms
and denies the Contingency Theory approach of Paul R. Lawrence and
Jay W. Lorsch. In Contingency Theory, the future of an organization is
not significantly determined by the long-term directions its managers give
it. Instead, what is critical is "the interplay between any major part of an
organization and its relevant external environment."[82] This interplay, quite
independent of the decision makers' intent, determines the directions the
organization will take in its development.

Assessed on these terms, Quaker growth exemplifies the Lawrence-
Lorsch thesis admirably. Here is an organizational entity with a radical
commitment to local autonomy—a commitment to the authority of
religious *experience* which is clearly far more fundamental than the structural orientations normally found in organizations. If any organization is
unlikely to change its structures under external pressure, it is Quakerism,
because of its extreme decentralization. Yet Quakerism does change; the
fundamental autonomy of the local meeting becomes a formality as the
community's innate drive for survival overcomes even its foundation in
religious experience.

Building on research by Lawrence E. Fouraker, Lawrence and Lorsch
differentiate type "T" groups from type "L." The former are marked by
independent members, responsive leaders, little hierarchy, and commit-

tee decisions. The contrasting "L" groups present responsive members, autocratic leaders, much hierarchy, and decisions which are made high in the hierarchy and passed down. "L" groups function best when there is some external threat, test, or competition against which the group must work.[83] Earliest Quaker meetings were clearly of the "T" group variety. The shift to an "L" type structure in face of external threat fits the Lawrence-Lorsch general hypothesis very nicely.

On a more specific level, however, the fit between Quaker history and Contingency Theory is not as tight as one might wish. Lawrence and Lorsch add to Fouraker the supposition that "L" groups cannot handle rapid environmental change with the adaptive abilities evidenced by "T" groups.[84] In the case of Friends, we have discovered that "T" groups were incapable of the effective and united inner discipline which persecution made necessary. The "L" organization pattern made survival possible.

A closer look at Quaker roots suggests that the Lawrence-Lorsch generalization that "T" groups are superior to "L" groups in adaptation to external threats is at least partially true. In the first ten years, when persecution itself was spasmodic and localized, Quakers seemed quite able to cope on a local level. The Quaker superstructure developed in response to persecution on a national level which was marked by uniform enforcement procedures. In light of the general principle that organizational development depends upon the interplay between organization and relevant external environment, one should not be surprised to discover that an environment of local and unsystematic persecution calls for the quick local adaptability of the "T" style group while an environment of systematic national persecution requires the disciplined and coordinated adaptation of the "L" type structure. A major change in the relevant external environment demands a major change in the corresponding internal structures for dealing with that environment.

A Look Ahead

We have now come to the end of the historical section of this study. Pursuit of the origins and development of Quaker decision making has revealed how the decision process evolved and how external pressures produced a structure contrary to the local experiential base of early Friends.

The chapters which follow focus on decision making by American Friends today. The method of study shifts. The object of attention becomes once more the "T" type structure of local entities which, in the United States where there was no such external threat as persecution, have retained their autonomy and guard it jealously against incursions from such higher bodies as the yearly meeting.[85]

The chapters ahead will explore Quaker decision making in much more concrete detail than was necessary in these historical chapters. These introductory chapters now stand simply as a historical backdrop for examination of contemporary decision making practices of Quakers in Philadelphia Yearly Meeting.

PART II

Contemporary

Chapter I

An Overview of Current Quaker Decision Making

Prescriptions for Good Quaker Practice

By now the reader is familiar with the general procedures for decision making which characterize Quaker practice. Concretely, what is that method like today? This introduction offers an overview of the rules observed as they might be discovered by someone reading standard Quaker sources. Subsequent chapters flesh out this skeleton on the basis of 150 interviews with anonymous Friends, personal observations, and further written materials. First, then, some excerpts from Quaker texts.

True to tradition, contemporary Friends are chary of "binding the Spirit" by supplying ironclad regulations. The official *Book of Discipline* of today's yearly meetings typically begins with a citation from the letter written in 1656 by the Quaker Elders of Balby, the citation setting the tone of the book as advice rather than regulation.

> Dearly beloved Friends, these things we do not lay upon you as a rule ✔ or form to walk by, but that all with the measure of light which is pure and holy may be guided, and so in the light walking and abiding these may be fulfilled by the Spirit—not from the letter, for the letter killeth, but the Spirit giveth life.[1]

The current *Book of Discipline* of Philadelphia Yearly Meeting* explains the process simply:

> Meetings for the transaction of business are conducted in the same expectant waiting for the guidance of the Spirit as is the meeting for wor-

---

* Held for one week each spring; all Friends in the Philadelphia area are invited to attend and to participate in area-wide decisions.

47

ship. Periods of worship, especially at the beginning and end, lift hearts and minds out of self-centered desires into an openness to seek the common good under the leadership of the Spirit of Christ. All matters are considered thoughtfully, with due respect to every point of view presented. When a course of action receives the general, though not necessarily unanimous, approval of the group, the presiding clerk formulates the sense of the meeting and it is recorded in the minutes. No vote is taken; there is no decision made by a majority, who override opposition. Action is taken only when the group can proceed in substantial unity.[2]

A typical set of suggestions for good procedure comes from London Yearly Meeting's *Book of Discipline:*

As it is our hope that in our Meetings for Discipline the will of God shall prevail rather than the desires of men, we do not set great store by rhetoric or clever argument. The mere gaining of debating points is found to be unhelpful and alien to the spirit of worship which should govern the rightly ordered Meeting. Instead of rising hastily to reply to another, it is better to give time for what has been said to make its own appeal, and to take its right place in the mind of the Meeting.

We ought ever to be ready to give unhurried, weighty and truly sympathetic consideration to proposals brought forward from whatever part of the Meeting, believing that what is said rises from the depths of a Friend's experience, and is sincerely offered for the guidance of the Meeting, and the forwarding of the work of the Church. We should neither be hindered from making experiments by fear or undue caution, nor prompted by novel suggestions to ill-considered courses.

Neither a majority nor a minority should allow itself in any way to overbear or to obstruct a meeting for church affairs in its course towards a decision. We are unlikely to reach either truth or wisdom if one section imposes its will on another. We deprecate division in our Meetings and desire unanimity. It is in the unity of common fellowship, we believe, that we shall most surely learn the will of God. We cherish, therefore, the tradition which excludes voting from our meetings, and trust that clerks and Friends generally will observe the spirit of it, not permitting themselves to be influenced in their judgment either by mere numbers or by persistence. The clerks should be content to wait upon God with the Meeting, as long as may be necessary for the emergence of a decision which clearly commends itself to the heart and mind of the Meeting as the right one.[3]

Individual writers concur with this picture of decision making. They expand upon the expectation that a final decision often is superior to the reflections of any individual in the group. James Walker, for example, tells us:

The business meeting is an occasion to use insight, and not an occasion for debate. After the facts of a situation are given and there has been time for consideration, members should try to state their judgment concisely and clearly. As this is done, new insights may come, and hopefully the final outcome will represent a group judgment superior to that of any one individual. Partiality has no place; rather we seek a decision that is right in the light of God's wisdom. After an individual has stated his own insight, his responsibility is over. Whether the meeting accepts or rejects the idea as given, the responsibility is on the group. If the group has reacted unfavorably, it will then endeavor to find a more creative approach.[4]

Thomas S. Brown, former clerk of Philadelphia Yearly Meeting, urges Friends to avoid "delivering remarks the meeting has heard many times before." One should ask oneself, "Is this repetition from frailty or from God?"

Brown urges that, instead of wasting the meeting's time with the polishing of the minutes which express the meeting's agreements, this editorial power should be entrusted to a committee, "for the Kingdom of God does not come minute by polished minute."

In a similar desire to keep the proceedings efficient, Brown urges careful preparation of the agenda by the clerk and respectful adherence to the agenda by participants in the meeting:

For the right holding of Meetings it is important for Clerks to have the known business meticulously prepared in advance of the session. Matters carried over from previous sessions should be noted and the persons who have been asked to take some action or to make a report should be reminded of the service expected. Members who wish to bring concerns before the Meeting should be urged to inform the Clerk in advance, and to have all possible relevant material in hand and to make their remarks brief and recommendations clear. If any member feels moved to rise in the Meeting to raise a major new concern, he should ask himself whether this matter might not better wait to receive the preliminary sifting of other Friends.[5]

The sweep of advice on how to participate, then, runs from mystical suggestions that one let God's promptings determine whether it is time to speak, to some very practical admonitions on the careful preparation of an agenda.

Meeting for business always begins with silence and closes in silence—a clear reminder that an atmosphere of worshipfully seeking God's will is to mark the gathering. Douglas Steere puts it well: "The Quaker meeting for business opens with an unhurried period of waiting

49

silence, and if the meeting is properly carried through, there emerges something of this mood of openness not to my wishes and my designs and my surface preferences but openness to the deeper levels where the Guide's bidding may have its way and where the problem may be resolved in quite a different way than had ever occurred to me."[6]

Examples of the Process

Even in such an atmosphere, differences of opinion may make agreement very difficult. In that case, no change is made until agreement is reached. An example is provided by Elton Trueblood using the apparently trivial conflict which arose over the enlargement of a burial ground:

> [T]he old burial ground in the meeting house yard was filled. Strong sentiment was expressed, when the matter was first discussed, both for and against the enlargement. Those in favor of enlargement pointed out the fact that many families could not be given space for burial without increasing the size of the plot and that failure to give space was unfair discrimination between families. Those opposed to enlargement showed that the proposed action would limit the playground of the school, situated on the same grounds, and that it made the section less desirable for residences. It must be understood that this subject was one on which many felt deeply. Those whose loved ones were buried in the tiny space allotted could not consider anything in connection with it dispassionately and it is not surprising that they could not. Others were equally unable to consider dispassionately anything affecting the life of the school children. To them it was a matter of interests of the dead against the interests of the living.
>
> Since a decision seemed impossible on the first evening, the clerk made no minute and the problem was allowed to rest a month. It was not until six months later, however, that the question was settled and settled in a satisfactory manner. The strong emotional tone wore off, and several tempered their former statements, until at last it was decided to make a sufficient enlargement of the grounds to care for those now in membership and to make other arrangements for the future so that the question would not again arise. This small enlargement was made in such a way as to do no harm to the playground, and all seemed to approve of the clerk's estimate of the sense of the meeting. Best of all the members did not feel that a weak compromise had been made, but rather that the very best plan had been followed.[7]

Nor is use of the method limited to exclusively Quaker groups. Burton R. Clark's description of faculty meetings at Quaker-sponsored Swarthmore College reveals the successful use of the method by a largely non-Quaker faculty:

50

The chairman would not commonly ask for a vote on an issue, and no one would rise from the floor to demand a count of hands or the use of a ballot. The expectation was that a common solution would arise through rational discussion, with each person first accepting for himself the rightness or appropriateness of a particular position. While the chairman and everyone else waited, there would be a search for the consensus; as the drift of opinion became clear, minority points of view often faded. The minority would see that the agreement necessary for policy and action lay in another direction, and if that direction seemed reasonable, they would go along with it. But a strong minority view that would not dissolve was taken seriously. Rather than vote it down, participants would continue the discussion or would table the issue so that further thought, discussion, and persuasion could take place outside the meeting room in the ensuing days and weeks. The matter might then be raised again at a subsequent meeting or, if a consensus was still missing, dropped.[8]

From the preceding citations, it is not difficult to detect a number of factors which seem characteristic of Quaker decision making. Stuart Chase[9] suggests nine such principles:

1. unanimous decisions—no voting;
2. silent periods—at start of meeting and when conflict arises;
3. moratorium—when agreement cannot be reached;
4. participation by all with ideas on the subject;
5. learning to listen—not going to meeting with mind made up;
6. absence of leaders—the clerk steers but does not dominate;
7. nobody outranks anybody;
8. factual-focus—emotions kept to a minimum; and
9. small meetings—typically limited numbers.

characteristic of Quaker decision-making

But which of these principles are fundamental and which derivative? Does Quaker unanimity entail the universal endorsement of decisions which it appears to? What goes on in the silences? Are all participants truly equal or only nominally so? Are emotions simply suppressed? To what extent does the method depend on the religious vision of Friends? Is a Quaker meeting for business really the leaderless body it appears?

In the chapters which follow we shall explore each of these questions in an attempt to bring the reader beyond the superficial comprehension which is the fruit of most of the descriptions one finds in print. Thus prepared, one should be able to attend Quaker business meetings with some sensitivity to the dynamics which are not otherwise obvious. Perhaps even some members of the Religious Society of Friends may find in these pages an occasional light on how his or her own meeting for business proceeds.

The sequence of topics deserves explanation. The writer has decided not to arrange all the important topics first (or last), with secondary matters placed in secondary positions. Instead, the focus is upon two central and subtle matters: the nature of unity in a decision and the systems of belief which seem to underlie successful use of the method. All other topics are introduced at points where they seem most apt for clarifying or being clarified by these central issues. For example, Chapter One discusses the atmosphere expected at a Quaker business meeting. This prepares the reader for an assessment of a primary issue, the nature of unity, which will be discussed in Chapter Two.

Chapter II

The Atmosphere of Confidence

Why Quakers Expect to Go Beyond Compromise

In the previous chapter, Elton Trueblood outlined the prolonged conflict within a monthly meeting over whether to expand the cemetery. He concluded his remarks with the observation that "best of all, the members did not feel that a weak compromise had been made, but rather that the very best plan had been followed."[1] A point of pride about Quaker decisions is that they occasion the emergence of such a higher synthesis of individual ideas. "The final result," comments S. B. Laughlin, "is not a compromise of conflicting views but a synthesis of the best thought of all—a case where two and two make five." Referring to Trueblood's decision about the cemetery, Stuart Chase explains, "The issue was not compromised but moved up to another level where a new plan was evolved—a plan in nobody's mind at the beginning of the discussion."[2]

An example may prove helpful. In 1967, a Quaker visiting a Philadelphia suburb made a public and fervent plea for a prompt end to the Vietnam War. In reaction, the local Quaker meeting house was defaced. At the meeting for business called to discuss the situation, many Friends thought that newspaper publicity should be sought; one felt strongly opposed. A number of prolonged silences followed. Finally, the Friend who had opposed the publicity suggested using the press to ask that area churches join a "paint-in" at the meeting house. This sort of publicity was readily endorsed by all.[3]

In his 1952 study of a Quaker meeting in Chicago, Glenn Bartoo states flatly, "In our experience compromise has never been resorted to."[4] Bartoo is, perhaps, a bit generous. This writer would rather say that compromise is the occasional exception to the rule.

Sometimes group pressure leads an individual to sacrifice what is best in favor of what is less embarrassing. As one Friend explained:

> The pressures on the dissenter are usually very strong; holding out takes great commitment. At our monthly meeting, the peace committee once wanted to put a picture in the paper of a previous vigil we had held against the Vietnam War. After three sessions, finally a compromise was accepted mainly because it was less offensive to those who were uneasy with opposition to the war. The compromise was just not as effective as the original proposal would have been.[5]

More generally, another Philadelphia Quaker commented, "There is the common tendency to turn to the lowest common denominator for a solution."

Friends sometimes, too, see a higher synthesis in outcomes where in fact neither side has been willing to budge. Burton Clark observes that the founders of Swarthmore were divided over whether it should be a college or a preparatory school. Instead of reaching a true higher synthesis, they agreed to open an institution that was both college and prep school, thus forcing the early educators to struggle over the question of priorities for a number of years.[6]

Granted the occasional failures, this observer was struck again and again by the efforts made in monthly meetings, at Philadelphia Yearly Meeting and Philadelphia Representative Meeting* to find solutions that would rise above the lowest denominator. This is as it should be. The goals of Quaker decision making are basically different from those of majority rule, a process to which most Americans are conditioned. The proposals made at the beginning of a discussion are thus usually seen by participants as starting points, not as finished products unsusceptible to modification.

At Representative Meeting, the spokesman for a committee making recommendations for remodeling an ancient building smiled at the end of his report and said: "Of course that's how *we* think it might be done. It might just be that Friends will have other ideas." For twenty minutes the meeting then discussed the pros and cons of the committee's suggestions with the committee's spokesman cheerfully revising the proposal

---

* Composed of individuals appointed by each monthly meeting to make decisions for the yearly meeting in months when the yearly meeting is not in session.

when the group moved towards options his committee had not presented.[7]

Our point here is that the attitude with which Friends approach a decision is different from that which prevails in the context of majority rule. In Quaker decision making, it generally is presumed that each participant seeks the best solution; it is also generally presumed that the group, by searching together, can reach such a correct solution. We shall see later how behavior which evidences attitudes contrary to this searching together suffers subtle but sharp sanctions. As a result, the common search for the best solution which is dismissed as pious rhetoric in the context of majority rule becomes an effective norm in the voteless Quaker world.

The attitude demanded of Friends is one of openness to one another's ideas—the ability to put aside pet notions in favor of the next person's insight. Francis, Beatrice, and Robert Pollard, writing in *Democracy and Quaker Method*, comment:

> It is true that such methods make great demands on those who practise them, and we must acknowledge that Friends sometimes take refuge from these demands in solutions which are little more than a mere shelving of them. The temptation to do this is the inevitable defect of the method's qualities. In experimenting with Quaker methods it would be necessary to understand this. The remedy is a deeper appreciation of the method. Those who dread the effects of candour in a Meeting are not giving that Meeting the opportunity which it needs to realise all the possibilities of its group life. Such a feeling is often an inverted fear of something within oneself, and the Meeting which is fully trusted by its members can do much to release them from that fear.[8]

Why There Are Few Shy Quakers

Release from fear, from shyness, from reluctance to express one's ideas is thus given high priority by Friends. In a sense, the conclusion reached by the assembly is a musical composition, and each participant has one note to contribute; if very many notes are missing, the theme loses its beauty and perhaps even becomes unrecognizable. In a very brief pamphlet on procedures at Quaker meetings, Thomas S. Brown still takes time to remark that "it is also of great importance that those Friends who feel they cannot speak acceptably and who are diffident about the significance of their share in the Meeting be encouraged to say what they can, remembering that the concerns they feel they present so haltingly may in fact point to issues needing the Meeting's consideration.[9]

James Walker urges the more vocal Friends to temper their remarks in order to encourage reluctant speakers: "Vocal members who tend to make up their minds quickly should make a special effort at self-restraint. Too frequently the leaders of the meeting seem to be making the decision without carrying with them the rank and file, who find it difficult to offer vocal opposition. Sometimes the quiet ones accept an unpalatable action because they have been unwilling to speak up. Under such circumstances they must accept at least part of the blame."[10]

One interview subject summed up his feelings this way: "With Friends, I know from experience that, even if I should say something foolish, nobody would make me feel embarrassed or think the less of me."

One of the quiet but constant reminders that this atmosphere will prevail is the Quaker style of discussion. We have seen a statement of London Yearly Meeting which counsels: "We do not set great store by rhetoric or clever argument. The mere gaining of debating points is found to be unhelpful and alien."[11]

Howard Brinton explains: "Eloquence which appeals to emotion is out of place. Those who come to the meeting not so much to discover Truth as to win acceptance of their opinions may find that their views carry little weight. Opinions should always be expressed humbly and tentatively in the realization that no one person sees the whole truth and that the whole meeting can see more of Truth than can any part of it."[12]

Public American rhetorical style in our own era is superficially similar to Quaker public speech—informal, devoid of oratorical flourishes, chary of blatant appeals to emotion—but one need only sit a short time in a Quaker meeting for business to recognize a deeper quality. Tentativeness and an artless willingness to face the weaknesses in one's position rather than to paper them over with distracting allusions are outstanding differences.

Sanctions against unacceptable rhetoric are subtle but effective. On the rare occasions when such speech happens, no comment is normally made; instead the discussion continues, the following speakers pointedly ignoring the offender's remarks. In the coffee break which next occurs, one is likely to overhear such wisps of conversation as, "John should know better than to speak like that," or, "If there's one thing that winds me down, it's the way Susan tries to get us all wound up." This is one form of the social sanctioning wryly described by Quakers as the "Philadelphia Treatment."

The Philadelphia Treatment also works in reverse. A Friend whose halting delivery or poor choice of words suggests that he or she is shy before groups will often find his or her theme picked up by one of the meeting's more respected and experienced members. In the coffee break or after the meeting, various Friends will stop the shy Friend to thank him or her for the insight. The shy Friend's contribution has thus been endorsed in public and in private. At the next meeting, the Friend is likely to be more confident.

Having made the above point, we feel duty bound to temper it a bit. The extent of shyness varies from one monthly meeting to the next. In one monthly meeting, the "old guard" may not be receptive to newcomers. In another, the "social activists" may be less than enthusiastic about the contributions of members who are "inadequately sensitive" to social issues. A dominant personality in yet a third meeting may keep would-be contributors from speaking their minds. Granted such failures, it is clear that Friends typically emphasize the importance of encouraging every participant in a meeting to feel that his or her contribution will be received with appreciation.

On Keeping Emotion in Its Place

Friends do have a problem when it comes to the expression of emotions. "Quakers hold back their emotions more than most people," volunteered one interview subject—an observation in which this observer would heartily concur. Because appeals to emotion are so out of place, Friends sometimes find it inappropriate to reveal their own inner feelings or to seek out ways of speaking which will let people know—in a non-rhetorical manner—the depth of their feelings. As a result, the emotional dimensions of topics sometimes do not get the frank attention they deserve because emotions are considered unworthy.

For example, a member of the Board of Directors of the American Friends Service Committee threw unexpected light on just this point. When asked whether a decision by the Service Committee to violate federal law and risk loss of tax exemption by shipping penicillin to the North Vietnamese was a good example of Quaker decision making, the following reply was made: "The penicillin decision was a good example of Quaker decision making. . . . But it's interesting that the decisions over which we have the most trouble are more 'average' issues: property, budgets, graveyards. On these matters, feelings are high. . . ."

In practice, Friends seem to have a scale for judging just how much personal feelings may be revealed. If an individual is generally quite cerebral and self-controlled, an occasional manifestation of personal feelings is accepted sympathetically. For example, a woman whose style of speech—in and out of meeting for business—was thoughtful and pleasantly off-handed, stood to complain that Quaker peace-promotion teams were being excluded from area high schools although army recruiters were welcomed with fanfare. She mentioned the pressures this put on young boys, her son among them. Her voice revealed deep grief and, on the verge of tears, she sat. A respectful silence was finally broken by speakers voicing agreement and offering practical steps the meeting might take.[13]

In this case, emotion seemed acceptable because it was rare. Clearly it was not the speaker's custom to speak this way—and because the emotions were not a substitute for reasonableness—even without her expression of feelings, the woman's concern was clearly in keeping with the Quaker commitment to peace education.

Three other members of the same meeting also spoke emotionally from time to time. In these cases, the contributions were received with limited sympathy. The remarks of the speakers who immediately followed the emotional contributions, the observations of Friends interviewed just after the meeting, and the examples cited during formal interviews when this problem was raised all indicated that sympathy was, at best, minimal. One person complained that such an individual got carried away all the time but just didn't "carry me along." The complaints seemed to focus on frequency and a tendency to let emotion obscure the issues.

It should also be noted that Friends seem to accept readily the simple statement that "this moves me deeply" as adding a factor of weight to an individual's remarks. This suggests once again that Friends are not opposed to emotions, not opposed to their having an important bearing on decisions. What seems important to Friends is that emotions be both deep and frankly recognized as emotions. Infrequency is a very handy measure of depth—hence the aversion to one who speaks this way all the time. But recognition is also important: I must know what my emotions are if I am to cope with them. So, too, must a group be aware of the feelings of its members. Hence, Friends are open to statements such as "I find this decision by the city makes me very angry," and to displays of emotion in which the feelings are revealed but kept under control of reason. In both situations, the emotions are recognized and can be dealt with thoughtfully. Although many Friends do seem to stifle their feelings, then, the mores of the meeting urge them to channel these emotions rather than to suppress them.

For those Friends who are aficionados of the "let it all hang out" school of human interaction—an approach somewhat popular among young adults in the community—the normal Quaker structure of channeled emotion seems stilted and even dishonest at times. However, all the Friends interviewed on this topic indicated a general sense of confidence in the meeting's willingness to sympathize with their own deep concerns.

This openness to deeply felt emotions is one more indicator of the warm subculture that seems to mark Quaker meetings. In order to foster that warmth, Howard Brinton suggests that a conscious effort be made at developing a real affection within the group, using any devices that will help it "become as much of a genuine unit, economically, socially, and in every other way, as its members desire." Quakers strive for increased "social solidarity." They lament the loss of such stimuli to fellowship as the old holiday week of yearly meeting which was held just before the plowing season so farm families could lodge in the homes of their Philadelphia brethren for full seven days, the latter closing their small shops for the duration.[14]

[margin annotation: holiday week]

When Confidence Fails

The atmosphere of respectful openness to one another is an essential element which is taken for granted by all the Quaker sources this writer has consulted. An example or two of what Quaker decisions are like without this atmosphere may be instructive.

Pendle Hill is a residential study center for adults—Friends and non-Friends—interested in thoughtful pursuit of social and religious questions traditionally explored by Quakers. In the late 1960s and early 1970s, even this institution was struck by the unrest common on campuses whose clientele were much younger. A member of the Pendle Hill Board of Directors describes the situation:

> For about five terribly difficult years, students—who are present from ten to twelve weeks—and staff—one year usually—demanded the right to participate in Board and Executive Committee decisions. The two bodies resented accepting them because the motivation was so clearly lack of trust, suspicion, desire of power. One man urged that there was no incongruity in disbanding Pendle Hill if some group there for twelve weeks should so conclude. They were finally allowed to be present in limited numbers—two staff, two students—and often revealed an inquisitorial belligerence. I recall one fellow's challenge of the treasurer. The treasurer finally was able to show him what the entries in the accounts stood for and he backed down, letting the atmosphere change.

And splits do exist within the Philadelphia Yearly Meeting. We shall discuss these in some detail later. For the moment, a single example may suffice. Especially troublesome is the case of inactive Friends from old Quaker families who are drawn to meeting for business on the occasion of some controversial issue—for example, contributing funds to a Black group which is demanding reparations, or removing the wall surrounding the cemetery where six generations of their ancestors are buried.

In such a situation this interviewer has had instances described where inactive Friends, rusty in Quaker methods, tend to become judgmental about the "insensitive" proposals of some of the meeting's active members. The latter are described (in private) as novices unused to Quaker ways. The active members, on their side, see a lack of commitment, a selfish prejudice in their normally inactive brethren. In such a situation, the externals of Quaker decision making may be observed, but our conversations with participants support our impression at such sessions that the dynamic of seeking a higher unity through receptiveness to that of God in the other was only minimally at work.

At times when such conflicts are especially vivid, some Friends find that the Quaker method is better used at the American Friends Service Committee—where the majority of employees who participate in decisions are usually non-Quakers—than at gatherings where all participants are Quakers but where genuine receptiveness to others is not achieved:

> I'd much rather work through a problem at the Service Committee than in a monthly meeting. I worry about the "sense of the meeting" approach in the Society of Friends. So often, the people making decisions don't have a lot in common—outlook, the endeavors in which they spend most of their time, etc. My monthly meeting suffered a shattering experience over the Black separatist groups. Lots of people came out of the woodwork who hadn't ever worshipped there. At AFSC, there are many viewpoints, but at least there is a context of effort to bring about improvement in the status of the neighbor and real interaction among the decision makers. You know this guy well enough to give serious hearing to his "far out" idea. Because of personal experience, we take one another seriously. My own ideas *have* changed on social issues because I've been nudged by colleagues with whom I interact so much.

The need for openness has some direct corollaries. Friends agree that their method is hamstrung whenever participants cannot be face-to-face: "On not really important issues, I admit that the phone or even correspondence may have to be used. But basically you need to look people in the eye to be sensitive to them."

Another corollary is that the topics with which a group can successfully deal are normally limited by the strength of the bonds of respect for one another which prevail within the community. We shall see more of this when we explore the role of the clerk in judging what items are ripe for the agenda.

But the purpose of this chapter is not so much to spell out details of Quaker procedure as to make clear to the reader the atmosphere that prevails in those situations where the Quaker method seems to work well. The emphasis is on acceptance of one another, mutual respect, avoidance of the manipulative conduct which rhetorical style often hides, a sense of the partiality of one's own insights, and one's dependence on searching together with the group for better conclusions than anyone alone could have attained.

With some notion of the general atmosphere as prelude, we are now in a position to explore one of our main topics, the nature of the unity involved in a decision.

Chapter III

No Decisions Without Unity

One major difficulty in assessing Quaker procedure is that no conventional term adequately expresses the phenomenon of decisional agreement in a Quaker meeting. Some describe all decisions as unanimous on the grounds that any objecting member could prevent action. But this is a misnomer because it implies that all participants are satisfied when a decision is reached—a point hardly true of many Quaker decisions. Other people speak of consensus, thereby underscoring that the bulk of those present agree even if one or two objectors remain. But this, too, is misleading. Quakers are simply not satisfied to know that even the overwhelming majority are in agreement.[1]

Given this verbal difficulty, many Friends adhere carefully to the term "unity" rather than "unanimity" or "consensus." This term, too, can be misleading if one makes it a synonym for unanimity. Unity, however, has the advantage of being widely used among Friends and has historical roots in the understanding that the one Spirit of Truth leads all to unite in what the Spirit reveals.[2] Hence, the common expression, "I can unite with what Friend Smith has said."

Another early Quaker term was concord. Edward Burrough exhorted his brethren in 1662 "to determine of things by a general mutual concord, in assenting together as one man in the spirit of truth and equity, and by the authority thereof."[3] The *Oxford English Dictionary* defines concordance in this same sense of harmonizing various accounts.[4]

The melodic image is useful. It suggests that the sort of agreement found in Quaker decisions is not an identity of view such that every participant ends up on the same note. Instead, they remain on different notes but blend them as the pianist blends conplementary notes into a chord.

Although this writer's preferred term would be concord, modern Quaker usage demands unity, a term of clear meaning to the Friend but open to misunderstanding by the outsider. However, the writer bows to current Friendly custom and speaks of Quaker unity in the discussion which follows.

Preliminary Discussion

In many Quaker decisions there are at least two stages of discussion. The preliminary stage follows initial presentation of both the problem and its possible solutions. At this point, participants often ask questions of the person who has made the presentation, offer tentative alternatives to the proposal, and even find themselves more in the posture of brainstorming than of making serious judgments. Remarks contrary to the proposal at such a time are taken to be exploratory. If the speaker decides to offer them seriously, he or she will have to raise them when the discussion gets to the more serious phase which precedes the declaration of unity by the clerk.

Transition from the preliminary to the serious phase is normally informal. An individual will begin to speak in a less tentative tone and others will follow this invitation and speak from their considered judgments rather than in an exploratory fashion.

At the time of transition, trial balloons are sometimes floated. An individual will offer a suggestion—perhaps a rejection of the basic proposal for a novel reason—and then sit back to see what response the idea draws from the group. Such a statement does not involve personal commitment to the idea one enunciates, although the neophyte observer could easily mistake the remark for a seriously-held objection. This observer did just that on a few occasions, only to discover in conversations after the session that the participants had generally read the remark as a testing of the waters.

The ability to differentiate tentative from serious and ambiguous remarks is important for all participants in the discussion, but especially for the clerk, whose duty it is to read the group and decide whether there is serious objection to the general direction in which discussion is moving.

Serious Discussion

As Friends begin to speak their serious conclusions, the tide will build.

Speakers will piggyback on the ideas of their predecessors. Listeners who find a speaker's remarks match their own feelings will follow his or her words with a chorus of "I agree" or "I can unite with that" or "that speaks my mind."

But sometimes several currents are running in the tide, pulling the meeting in two or more directions. Or there may be no tide or current at all: even after discussion, the participants may find that no option draws them into unison. In either of these situations, discussion continues until a dominant position emerges or until, at the suggestion of the clerk or some other participant, there is agreement that no conclusion can be reached for now. In this case, the matter is postponed: "It is the clerk's task within the plexus of this corporate exercise either to find a resolution with which the assembled Friends can largely agree or to follow the Quaker rule, 'when in doubt, wait'. In the latter case the minute might read: 'Friends could not reach clarity on a resolution of the issue in this meeting and it was agreed to postpone that matter until the following monthly meeting'."[5]

If, however, the tide is running in a particular direction, the clerk is expected to make a judgment that the group is now ready for agreement and to propose a tentative minute embodying the agreement as the clerk understands it from listening to the discussion.

Dissent from a Proposed Minute

When the clerk proposes a minute, each member of the assemblage has two quite different questions to ask. First, does the proposed minute catch the drift of discussion? If the answer is no, then this opinion is expected to be raised. One occasionally hears such a paradoxical remark as: "If it please the clerk! Although the minute pleases me, I suspect it says a bit more than Friends are willing to say." More typically, the objection will be phrased; "Well I, for one, would be uncomfortable with such a minute. And, from what I've heard, many others in the room would be uncomfortable, too."

Discussion follows such an objection, with various Friends stating how they respond to the minute as an expression of the group's will. The clerk rephrases or withdraws the minute if need be.

If the clerk is adept at chairing the meeting—more on this in a later chapter—such misreading of the group's leanings is relatively rare. Under an experienced clerk, therefore, each participant is much more likely to move to a second question. Although the minute reflects the trend of the group, is each member comfortable with that trend? If the answer is no, one may choose to rise in order to speak against the minute. Perhaps the group has not considered adequately a point which has hidden import. After one speaks, others will agree or disagree and, once any new discussion has run its course, the clerk will either again propose the original minute or offer a substitute depending on whether the discussion revealed a shift in preferences. It is often the case that one person's statement of misgivings leads others to reassess their judgments, giving more prominence to matters they had initially dismissed.

But suppose the group remains unmoved by one person's uneasiness. Given the folklore of Quaker dissent, the answer is simple: if the person can't agree, the group is unable to proceed. The realities, fortunately, are much more subtly adapted to the complexities of human disagreement. For example, opposition to an advertisement in the *New York Times* calling for the impeachment of the president is quite a different category from opposition to starting a cleanup project at 9 A.M. instead of 9:30 A.M. on Saturday. In Quaker decision making, a whole spectrum of dissent is available. The paragraphs which follow indicate some typical points on the spectrum.

"I Disagree but Do Not Wish to Stand in the Way"

In many instances the point of disagreement, for one reason or another, is not strong enough to merit standing in the way of the decision. For religious reasons, a person may prefer the judgment of the group as "sincere seekers after the divine leading" to the individual judgment. In more secular terms, an individual may recognize the possibility that everyone else is right, or that an important principle is or is not involved.[6]

This is the level at which, in practice, most dissent is expressed. The meeting is left aware of the dissenter's opinion, yet the dissenter has indicated a wish not to keep the matter from moving forward.[7] Equivalently, the objector has thus endorsed the action of the group by implying that *in his or her own judgment* the objection is not serious enough to prevent action.[8]

The dissenter has thus put him or herself in a psychologically peculiar but liberating situation. The individual can leave the meeting with a sense of integrity ("I never approved the proposal. There was no compromise of my own belief, my own leaning.") because he or she did not, after all, pretend to endorse the group's choice. But at the same time, the individual also feels some sense of responsibility because, "I could have stopped or at least delayed the action, but I didn't." Therefore, the individual tends to take some responsibility for the decision, even to feel some obligation for making it work out well in practice. We shall explore this matter in more depth later on.

In Quaker decisions, this moment of withdrawing one's opposition—though not one's disagreement—so the meeting may proceed is a very important way of preventing polarization and its exercise, therefore, is virtually an art form of graciousness. Paradoxically, some Friends make a point of being especially strong in their criticism of a proposal because they know that, if the proposal is accepted by the group, they will have this moment to withdraw their opposition and therefore to prevent their harsh statements from working permanent division into the community. Here is an example which indicates the importance of the withdrawal.

At the 1975 session of Philadelphia Yearly Meeting, a major bone of contention was the size of the budget for the Yearly Meeting staff in the year ahead. A small but vocal group from a monthly meeting claimed to be dissatisfied with the emphasis of the Yearly Meeting staff on social work in the Philadelphia metropolitan area—work of little service to meetings like their own outside the metropolitan area. The treasurer of the group complained that the budget for the Yearly Meeting had been enlarged every year for the last ten years and that it would be necessary to fire the monthly meeting's one full-time employee to meet their proportional share of the proposed Yearly Meeting budget. Prolonged discussion revealed that the bulk of the speakers did not concur with the monthly meeting's desire to cut the Yearly Meeting's budget.

The evening was wearing on. The clerk reminded all of the shortness of time and, picking up an earlier suggestion that it might be possible for financially strong monthly meetings to absorb a larger proportion of the increased budget than financially weak meetings. He remarked that it was clear the budget had been approved but also that the Yearly Meeting had a responsibility to be concerned about the unhappiness of displeased meetings and that therefore a meeting ought be held later on to decide whether costs could be partly absorbed by meetings which felt they were financially stronger.

From the floor came the cry, "I fail to see how the Yearly Meeting has approved the budget when a number of us do not approve the budget."

The clerk replied that, in the judgment of the clerk, the only major point of contention was that of distributing the financial burden. Since this would now be put off until a later meeting for settlement, the matter of the budget was in fact settled; the matter of its mode of appropriation would be settled at a subsequent meeting.

For the moment, the clerk's reply silenced, although it did not satisfy, the objector. The objecting Friends had been as much upset about the way Yearly Meeting expenditures were focused on social projects in Philadelphia as over the added financial burden and the clerk's declaration seemed to ignore this concern.[9]

Conversations with those present cast light on Quaker custom. One man of many years' experience indicated that the clerk had clearly been right in saying that the general feeling was in favor of the budget, but that the clerk seemed to have stretched his role as far as you can take it in moving things too rapidly to a conclusion before the dissatisfied members had withdrawn their objection. A number concurred in the observation that the size of the assembly—several hundred people—and the lateness of the hour had led the clerk to move too fast. A few—one on the floor of the meeting the next day—complained that the clerk was misapplying Quaker procedures.

In interviews some weeks later, however, individuals who had initially objected to the budget felt "very content with the outcome." They didn't really want to block the budget; they wanted to serve notice of its questionable dimensions for the monthly meetings. The monthly meeting the objection came from was "rather suspect among Friends anyway" and thus drew little real sympathy for its objections. One observer commented:

> The clerk read the mood of the house perfectly well. If he made any mistake at all, it was in letting the press of time short circuit the normal procedure. He might better have declared that "Friends seem to be at an impasse" and asked for a few moments of silence. Or he could have indicated he was unable to make a minute and asked whether the Meeting wished to drop the next day's agenda until this matter might be resolved. In either case, the objecting Friends, having made their point, would have indicated a desire not to stand in the way. But he moved too quickly and took away their chance to withdraw their objections.

The clerk's speed thus seemed to lead to a sense of polarization in the group by depriving the dissidents of their moment of reconciliation. Given the number of Friends with strong opinions on the subject even months after this event, it would seem that the ramifications were not ephemeral.[10] Withdrawal of objections is far more than a ritual; it truly liberates the meeting to go forward and prevents the polarization that normally arises at the moment of voting when one side becomes victor, the other vanquished. In the Quaker system, such a moment does not normally arise because those who have been unable to sway the group have the opportunity to join it. In joining the group, they truly do free it to act.

"Please Minute Me as Opposed"

One step further along the spectrum of dissent is a practice much less common among Friends—and therefore much more significant—the request that one can be "minuted as opposed." In this case, the objector wishes that the minute expressing the sense of the meeting should note his or her disagreement. Although fairly common in the past, the procedure is unfamiliar to many Quakers today. Its use leaves the meeting free to proceed but also tends to make the group more reluctant than if the objector had stopped short of asking to be listed in the minute as opposed. An example from the Board of Directors of Pendle Hill, the Quaker adult education facility outside Philadelphia, may be helpful:

> We had a problem at Pendle Hill over whether to permit cohabitation of unmarried students and/or faculty. In both cases, remember, we are talking of people older than college age. After lengthy consideration, the Board settled on a policy in which we did not approve such cohabitation but did give the administration discretion in exceptional cases to allow it.
> One Board member wanted his name recorded in dissent in the minute. It was necessary for the clerk to explain to some Friends that such was an appropriate procedure. Four more Friends then asked that their names be added to his. This was a sizable number; yet none desired to prevent the movement forward.

The decision drew wide notice among Philadelphia area Friends. The notations of dissent made the action seem experimental, tentative, hesitant. Curiously, the action did not stir the amount of criticism among Quakers one might have expected, perhaps precisely because its painful uncertainty was so clearly underscored.[11]

Depending upon the circumstances, the request that one be "minuted as not united" with the decision can make a group much more hesitant to go forward than the mere withdrawal of objection. In both cases, however, the objector explicitly indicates that the objection should *not* stand in the way.

"I Am Unable to Unite with the Proposal"

Next on the spectrum is a situation in which a person is simply "unable to unite" with a proposal in such a basic way that he or she is unwilling to stand aside and let the meeting move forward. In such a situation, the normal procedure is to delay action until a later time. If time is short or the objection seems frivolous, the clerk or another Friend may appeal to the objector to withdraw the objection or to consent to be minuted as opposed.[12]

If there is a delay, all take time to reflect again on their positions. Discussions may also occur among those who participated in the recent meeting. The clerk and those highly respected by the objector may make strong efforts to understand the roots of the objection. This is one form of what Quakers call "laboring with Friend X."

At the meeting which follows, very often agreement is possible. The objector's problem has been traced to something nonessential in the proposal and the proposal has been adjusted accordingly. Or the objector has come to see that his or her unhappiness is not so profound as originally thought and is now willing to stand aside. Often, too, the objector is now able to stand aside because he or she is confident that trusted members of the meeting have understood his or her point of view and, having thought it through conscientiously, still do not agree. The individual's respect for their judgments makes it easier to let the decision go forward. The person can, of course, still choose not to unite with the decision, although the social pressure to unite grows with each delay and each discussion with a respected Friend. If the individual does not unite, the group may continue to delay or, thinking the objections frivolous, proceed anyway. Delay is the much more likely course. Many an interview subject has summed up the likely outcome of a conflict within his or her meeting with the remark, "We won't solve this one until we have a good Quaker funeral or two."

Absence

Our spectrum is complicated by the Friend who does not attend a meeting at all. The cause is normally no more than disinterest or the press of other responsibilites. But a Friend who is regularly a member of the group but absents him or herself at a time of critical decision becomes conspicuous. A Friend absented herself from a Quaker school's board meeting where she knew it would be decided to invite parents of non-Quaker students to join the Board. "If I had gone," she confided to another board member, "I would have just had to object. So I didn't go." Her absence was felt by all. But the Board went ahead with its decision. Deliberate absence can, then, have multiple meanings. Even when it signifies deep disagreement with a proposal, it does not necessarily block action.

Intangible Factors Affecting the Impact of Dissent

It might be helpful here to return to the spectrum of possible modes of dissent and indicate likely outcomes. Basically, the group can be expected to go ahead at once if the objector follows the typical approach of stating his or her unease but affirming a desire not to stand in the way. The same is true even if he or she asks to be minuted as opposed, although it seems that the group will proceed in much more chary fashion. (This is based on sparse evidence; current cases are extremely rare.) If the individual feels simply unable to unite, the group will normally delay action.

But for how many meetings will the group delay action on one subject? To answer this question, we must introduce a new and complicated set of factors. In practice, the group's willingness to delay is a function of the apparent importance of the objector's objection—how deeply a matter of principle is it? The group's readiness to delay also depends on its respect for the objector. What is the individual's reputation for wisdom or spiritual sensitivity or expertise in the area under consideration? Yet a third factor is time. The more urgent the matter, the more highly regarded the objector needs to be.[13] And, of course, how many objectors are there? Fifteen out of 100, even if they do not carry much weight as individuals, form a significant group.

In a sense, these factors are a social scientist's nightmare. The relative significance of each factor depends in each situation upon the entire set of relationships existing at a given moment within the group under consideration. Any single factor—size of the minority, reputation of the objector(s), pressure of time, importance of the issue to the objector(s), importance of the issue to the most respected spokesmen for the dominant side—can be significant enough to control the outcome in one situation, but unimportant in the next.

Chapter IV

Belief Systems Underlying
Quaker Decision Making

Myth from a Social Scientific Viewpoint

Quaker understanding of how unity is reached and the significance of their decisions can be confusing. One says the group has reached Truth, meaning Truth is the guiding light of Jesus Christ. Another finds in Truth the best aspirations of man but dismisses references to Christ as "baggage from another age" when people didn't know better. If four Quakers agree that Christ is the Truth which guides Friends, then for one this means that Christ is the historic Jesus, for another a name for the Creator, for the third an impersonal force, and for the fourth a euphemism for the relief one feels when one has tried hard to be honest in making a choice.

No matter how contradictory the language sounds at first, it all points to a mutually-shared event: Friends experience something special and invoke some privileged explanation to indicate why their type of decision is different from ordinary ones. They find an authenticating dimension outside the mechanics of the process. One Friend, a professional political scientist himself, commented: "I doubt that a common goal plus acceptance of the rules is enough. . . . There is need of a bona fide religious myth, a mysticism, to which people really feel subordinate."

Before we explore the alternative Quaker myths, perhaps it would be helpful to explain our use of the term myth. A myth, as defined by Karl Rahner and Herbert Vorgrimler, is "an intellectual construction that fuses concept and emotion into an image."[1] The myths with which we are concerned are "collective representations"[2] rather than the product of a single mind. Explaining religious myth, Rahner comments:

> If we assume that every concept bearing upon a metaphysical or religious reality, remote from direct experience, must work with a sensible image . . . which is not the original phenomenal form of that reality but is arrived at from elsewhere; if we further assume that this image . . . is not a static "picture" but a dramatic representation—an event—or can be developed into one, and that such a thing can then be called a mythical representation: then every metaphysical or religious utterance is a mythical one or can be interpreted in mythical terms.[3]

In our usage, a myth is a concrete embodiment of beliefs which makes sense out of religious phenomena for a group of believers. Myths can convey truth or falsehood or both. They are worth studying because they can help explain why those who hold them act as they do.

Let us now look at the second principal topic of this essay, the major competing Quaker myths, and see how they buttress Quaker meetings for worship and meetings for business.

As a prelude, we should underscore that the following are pure positions. They were distilled from many interviews with people who tend to hold positions like these or combinations of these or, in some cases, to shift positions according to the situation.

Christocentrism

The Christocentric Quaker is easiest for typical Americans to understand. He or she shares with most American Protestants a conviction that the historical Jesus was in some way the Son of God, that the Gospels express his teaching in a privileged fashion, and that he is active in our world today as its Lord.[4] To be sure, the Gospels are only one channel to that Lord and cannot supersede his present revelation in individual prayer and the meeting's worship. For the same Spirit of Jesus the Inner Light is found in both. Decisions reached in the Life are guaranteed by the promised guidance of Jesus: "Where two or three are gathered in my name, there am I in the midst" (Matthew 18:20). Beneath the mutual trust at a Friends meeting is the conviction that each person present is "indwelt by the spirit of 'God the Father of our Lord Jesus Christ' " (Ephesians 1:3).[5]

Christocentric Quakers can be readily divided into two subgroups. The first tend to be fundamentalist in their theology. They take Scripture literally: creation was in six days; Jesus uttered each saying attributed to him exactly as recorded; and the details of each miracle in Scripture are historically precise. Although all age groups are represented here, many adults among these individuals tend to have been uninfluenced by the science versus the Bible dispute of their college days and are unaware of modern biblical research.

The second subgroup of Christocentric Quakers tends to hold theological positions in keeping with modern mainstream Protestantism and Catholicism. For such a Quaker, the Jesus of history is the same person as the Inner Light of today, but the literal acceptance of events and statements in Scripture must be modified by understanding the literary genres employed in each passage, ancient notions of history, et cetera. In practice, although Scripture and present revelation are both channels to God, the latter are often much more reliable indicators of divine guidance than Scripture.

This subgroup seems to include few young adults and few elderly adults. Its members appear in the thirty-five to sixty-five age range, given our interviews and observations of references to God in meetings for worship and meetings for business. The group is more in touch with modern scholarship than either its fundamentalist or its universalist confreres.[6]

Universalism

Universalist Quakers seem by far the majority group in Philadelphia Yearly Meeting. They, too, can be subdivided into two groups. The first subgroup would include all those who hold for some exterior guiding principle—the "Other"—beyond man's life. Jesus was an especially great man, an exemplar for us of devotion to God. But he was not God and his death was not salvific. Man is good by nature; he needs divine guidance but not redemption from a state of sin.

The divine Other—be it personal or impersonal[7]—does indeed afford guidance to those who truly seek it. Such guidance is received in private reflection and in meeting. Said one Friend, "The assumption among Quakers is that there's something more than mankind—call it God, ultimate reality or whatever else—a something deeper than man which does guide if we're open to it." For such a Quaker, Christian language is bound up in time. That is, traditional Quaker formulas reflect the naively literalist vocabulary of the age in which Fox emerged and therefore the terminology in which he had to speak.[8] Thus, the Society of Friends is Christian by accident.[9]

In spite of the chasm of belief between this subgroup and the holders of a Christocentric position, these universalists share with their Christocentric brethren a willingness to see in the experience of the Inner Light a manifestation of a divine guidance which claims allegiance. Decisions reached in an atmosphere of worship are just as preferable to these Friends as to the Christocentric sort; their sense of a special obligation to obey such religiously achieved decisions appears equally strong.

A second subgroup under the universalist banner might well be labelled humanists. These are people who tend to translate all "God talk" into elevated allusions to the fundamental aspirations and potential of human-beings-at-their-best. As Stanley Ellin wrote in a letter to the *Friends Journal*, "Where most Christians would interpret the message, 'I and the Father are one,' as defining the nature of Jesus, for us it expresses the divine potential in all men."[10] To these Friends, religious language is appropriate for enshrining human potential so long as it is not taken literally. Here are two examples:

> What it is important to emphasize is the . . . desire [of all Friends] to meet on every occasion in a spirit which seeks conclusions that are constructive, wise and loving, or as some would prefer to say, that are consistent with the will of God.[11]
> One of the immediate and important objects of a Quaker meeting for worship is to create a Christian fellowship. . . . if the Quaker meeting never produced any other results save those arising from an increase in human fellowship, the meeting would be justified.[12]

Numbered among these universalist Friends are Jewish agnostics, Buddhists, and Hindus who find in Quakerism "no religion at all, but a form of humanism concerned with ethics and the improvement of the human lot."[13]

Of all the groupings, this humanitarian-universalist type is the most elusive to categorize. The experience of being gathered, for example, is deeply meaningful to some humanitarian-universalists—a moment when each is in touch with his or her "best self." For such people, decisions taken in a gathered condition carry a heavy sense of obligation without the impairment of individual freedom since—shades of Rousseau—each individual is only obeying his or her best self or obeying a higher standard which the group finds rather than creates. Writes Glenn Bartoo: "The goals are *above* the *group* as well as above the individual. Hence, individuals don't perceive the group as interfering with their individual freedom."[14] Friends the writer has interviewed who expressed leanings in this direction seemed emphatic about having an obligation to carry out group decisions reached in the Life. Although this observer does not have enough information to indicate with confidence whether their sense of obligation matches that of those of Christocentric or Other-oriented Friends, the sense of obligation appears less strong.

For a second subgroup in this humanitarian-universalist category, the experience of being gathered is obviously much less significant. Some avow that they find it a curious group phenomenon and suggest telepathy, extra-sensory perception, or other psychic phenomena as the explanation.[15] When asked about a sense of obligation to obey a group decision, they allude to common sense and a desire to trust the corporate wisdom, but not to a special binding character the decision may carry, even if reached in a deeply religious atmosphere. People with this leaning tend to em-phasize that gathered meetings for worship are very uncommon. One, a Friend for only three years, said she had never experienced such a meeting. As for the gathered meeting for business, such Friends are like-ly to remark that it happens so infrequently that one need not bother to worry about it.

The universalist Quaker, whether Other-centered or humanitarian, can be of any age. People in middle and old age of this persuasion often indicate a knowledge of the old science versus the Bible disputes. Typically college-educated, they find Quaker universalism a "haven for the doub-ting Thomases of a scientific age."[16] One Christocentric Friend explained: "The triumvirate of Darwin, Marx, and Freud led Quakers in the 40's, 50's and 60's to favor more a psychological than a 'divine inspiration' explana-tion of the deep experiences of Quakers. Now, with discovery that it's safe, respectable again to be a believer, there's a new turn to explicit faith especially among Friends who stay in touch with the educational scene."[17]

One must be careful not to imply that Quaker universalism is a relative-ly recent phenomenon. Elias Hicks, leader of one party in the great Quaker schism of 1827, seemed committed to an Other-centered universalism.[18] However, the Orthodox party of that same schism fell under universalist influence at the turn of the present century under the inspiration of the Quaker philosopher-historian Rufus Jones. Interview subjects in their seventies and eighties spoke of a personal commitment to universalism going back to their childhood.

Superficially, at least, the most senior and the newest adherents to Quaker universalism are much alike. Both believe in a divine dimension of life but without attributing much reality to traditionally Christian Quaker language. But the similarity is not complete. Middle-aged and elderly Friends show an optimism about the human condition and the world's future which their younger coreligionists do not share: An experienced clerk commented:

> In the young Friends and attenders* nowadays you find a distinctive cast of mind. Many are radically pessimistic: man isn't good. This is very different from traditional Quaker optimism; it seems to come from the experience of the Viet Nam War. For these young Friends, Christianity is seen in a very negative light: Christianity is divisive, . . . has occasioned many wars, has led to persecutions, has kept well-intentioned men apart. These younger folks are reluctant to take the Christocentric path. Universalism seems much more appropriate to them.

Social Activism

Although it would be convenient if we could limit Quaker myths to the Christocentric-universalist spectrum, neither our interviews nor written materials will allow for such clean categories neatly grouped around the question, Who is God? Among Friends there is a sizable group which is more concerned with healing God's children than with who God is. Said one woman: "I find I'm more interested in justice than in beliefs. My 'worship' is more in service than in the meeting house." Walter Rauschenbush's Social Gospel movement, emanating from the University of Chicago in the 1920s and 1930s, was a significant support of this trend among Quakers. More recently, many in this group have joined Friends after being attracted to nonviolent Quaker practice through the American Friends Service Committee.

We repeat that we are talking of pure types here and that Friends who are social activists *also* belong somewhere on the Christocentric-universalist spectrum. But the social activist myth itself is important because it uses Quaker decision making without recourse to any of the more formally theological positions. Quakers who emphasize this social activist understanding of their religion tend to be much more pragmatic about the significance of Quaker decisions. One Friend commented, "Seeking unity because you make a bigger impact if you all go at something together" is quite different from seeking unity because divine guidance can be found there.

The social activist type lacks much of the sense of the authority of decisions which we saw in the Christocentric or the universalist Other-centered type. With the universalist-humanist type is shared a desire to trust the group's insight or to increase impact through acting in a united

---

* Attenders are individuals who come to a Friends meeting but have not become formal members.

fashion. But the specially binding character of the decision reached in a religious atmosphere is not significant for such a Friend. Interestingly, a number of interview subjects indicated that decisions regarding social action tend to be less frequently reached in a religious atmosphere in their own monthly meetings, sometimes with the rather feeble excuse that "social issues seem too complex for divine guidance." The writer did *not* observe this at meetings he attended. However, the attitude if true may reflect the needs of the social activists who become prominent in these decisions and see no value in moving to a religious level.

Democracy

For years, Quakers have prided themselves on having a system of "radical democracy"[19] in the sense that all present are of equal worth in the eyes of God and have an equal right to participate. This love for democracy has been carefully balanced with a disclaimer such as this one provided by Howard Brinton: "In the voting method of 'one man, one vote' the opinion of the foolish or indifferent counts for as much as that of the wise, interested, or responsible. In the Quaker meeting for business, wise and foolish are both listened to, but the contribution of each to the final judgment has at least an opportunity to be gauged in proportion to its wisdom."[20]

The American democratic myth has had its impact on Quaker practice, however. Some Friends bridle at the very notion that one participant ought to have more influence than the next. Others point out that some of their weaknesses in effectively using Quaker decision making processes arise because of the American political heritage: "Most of us in this meeting are convinced Friends. We were not born as Quakers but joined as adults. We don't leave it all behind when we become Friends."

Democracy, when carried to the full, can radically change the meaning of the Quaker decision. A Quaker social scientist who is now disaffected from Friends and sees in their process "nothing special" asserted: "The idea that we can find a specific choice which all can accept is akin to the majority rule premise that the decision will not be so repugnant that the losing voters will have to withdraw." He indicated that Quaker decisions contrary to his leaning drew from him the same kind of acceptance as majority rule decisions: "If a system is fair, I am bound by its outcomes."

Such an individual has little motivation to put aside personal preference in favor of the group's leading or to make an enthusiastic contribution to a decision which he had not favored. Comments one Friend:

> Some Friends seem to see democracy as the hallmark of Friends decision making. They hold for the "one-man-one-vote" principle. Their use of "democracy" is a substitution of equal political power for the Quaker fundamental insight that God can speak in anyone. It's easy to fall into this trap. After all, democracy is an "in" word. Surely we don't want people to think of us as "antidemocratic"! But the person who sees our method as "pure democracy" has missed its root principle. At root, we are involved in an exercise of obedience, of denial of self-will, of seeking truth in contradistinction to our own personal or group interest.

It is this writer's impression that the democratic myth among Friends is generally undeveloped, unreflective, and an often unrecognized symptom of the ambient political culture. As such it rarely reaches the conscious expression of the Quaker social scientist quoted just above. Instead, it tends to coexist with one of the other self-understandings discussed in this chapter and to emerge spontaneously, for example, when an individual finds that his or her opinion seems to merit less consideration than that of another.

Ambiguity

We have mentioned that each of the above self-understandings is a pure position. For any given individual, a combination of positions is very likely. With some, even prolonged interviews failed to reveal the particular meaning a Friend assigned to such common Quaker terms as Inner Light or the divine. Unwillingness to share deep personal experiences accounts for some of this lack of clarity. One elderly Quaker was initially very strong in his assertion: "I have never spoken in meeting under the 'leading' of the Spirit. All I do is use my reason and speak what makes sense." A little later he suggested: "It's funny; when I speak at meetings for worship, I always seem to just find myself on my feet." Ten minutes later, when the interviewer asked about the nature of a gathered meeting for worship, the Friend smiled and commented, "Well, it sure seems the group is present to what people call the Spirit."

Interviews of this sort suggest not only the superiority of the open-ended interview over the questionnaire for obtaining certain information, but also the ambiguous, even contradictory quality of the levels of understanding within a given individual.

Subtle shifts in use of language and concept are common. Asked whether a person can be a Quaker and an atheist, one senior Friend replied: "I wouldn't see the consistency, myself. But I'd also be skeptical at face value about accepting a person's self-description as an atheist. Of course, I'm not sure how many folks would accept my notion of God as theism, either."

Such encounters reminded the interviewer of Thomas O'Dea's observation that the Mormons, who like the Quakers of Philadelphia Yearly Meeting lack a professional clergy, are thereby deprived of consistent theological language which the education of clergy produces. Observed O'Dea, "In terms of theology, the church is governed not only by laymen, but also by amateurs."[21]

Quaker Myths in Perspective: Primacy of the "Event"

One evening, the writer was sharing supper with two Friends in their late seventies. He mentioned he was curious about how Friends understood God. One of his companions paused and remarked: "Well now, I guess I don't really know. I know what I think." Then, turning to his comrade, he said: "Thee and I have been worshipping together for almost fifty years. I don't know what thee thinks about God. I don't think we've ever talked about it." The other grave Friend agreed, adding: "I really don't think it matters much, either. If thee shares the experience in the worship, it doesn't much matter how thee puts it into words."

This Friend's observation brings things into salutary focus. Quakerism has always been a community without creed precisely because it did not need a creed. Unlike other faiths, Quakerism builds all on the experience of the gathered meeting. Together Friends experience something beyond themselves, superior to the human pettiness that marks ordinary life. One may find in this experience the Spirit of Christ, another the Divine Person, a third the force behind the universe. No matter how they explain the experience to themselves, the event which they share is paramount. They stand in awe before it, finding that it dominates their conduct as they meet together to make a decision. And the event demands that, in reaching that decision, they should sacrifice self-interest and seek after a higher truth than what they have individually achieved.

The whole emphasis of Quaker decision making as we have now sketched it draws upon this experience. Because Friends differ in their understandings of the experience, the devices used in the meetings are subtle invitations to reenter the experience rather than formal reminders of Quaker belief. The opening and closing silences and the moments of special reflection at times of impasse or conflict all recall those present to the experience, each remaining free to enter the experience through his or her own understanding. Even such archaisms as use of "thee"[22] for "you" serve to remind the participant that the context is a distinctively Quaker one, different from worldly procedure. Quaker authors, whether they speak of spiritual empiricism or practical mysticism, constantly emphasize the centrality of the religious experience and disparage such appealing notions as democracy as threats to the Quaker way.[23]

When asked whether this sort of understanding is necessary to successful use of the process, Friends point to the weakness of the process whenever participants are permitted to hold out for their personal desires. A number of Friends active in the American Friends Service Committee suggested, for example, that the process becomes distorted at budget-making sessions when individuals tend to put primacy on their own special area and hold out for full funding. "When a lower-level AFSC committee starts to divvy up the financial pie, he who pushed the hardest often gets his way."[24]

Others discussed the difficulty that women's lib absolutists and Black activists present to the Service Committee. Such individuals sometimes want to caucus prior to meetings so they can plan strategy. They "tend to resign from the Service Committee in frustration" because the Committee doesn't "put their concern ahead of everything else." In short, they are committed to concrete goals and unwilling to "put themselves under the discipline" of a community for which "religious events," not these goals, are normative.

This writer found many Friends suggesting that people whose entry into the Quaker community was occasioned by the Vietnam War and other issues of the late 1960s will "either discover Friends' worship or leave." Along this same line, the researcher noted that interview subjects who came to Quakerism through the AFSC and have remained for many years often speak strongly of the importance of Quaker worship in their personal lives.

Levels of Unity: A Religious Dimension Not Always Desirable

We have previously noticed that the "meeting for business is, in essence, the meeting for worship focused upon specific matters."[25] The initial and concluding moments of silent worship are reminders of this intent. Tied to the worshipful atmosphere is an "expectation of corporate guidance."[26]

The religious tone of a meeting for business can run a spectrum from the merest formality to an extraordinary quality very significant to the decision being taken. On the formalistic end of the spectrum, the initial silence seems about as significant as the chaplain's invocation at the Democratic National Convention.[27] At the opposite pole, however, one thinks of occasional meetings—or parts of meetings—when the comments of individual speakers were followed by long spontaneous silences for prayer and the observer felt himself drawn into the group's profoundly worshipful seeking. This gathered or centered or covered condition has already been described as it appeared in its more typical Quaker context, the meeting for worship.

Such a worshipful situation is occasionally accompanied by surprising shifts of position, either by individuals or by the entire group. An example from the American Friends Service Committee may be helpful. In an interview, one former AFSC staff member recalled:

> In 1948, there were 750,000 refugees on the Gaza Strip; the new state of Israel had just been established. The UN asked AFSC to take responsibility for feeding, housing, etc. At the meeting of the AFSC Board of Directors, all speakers said the work needed doing, but *all* agreed it was just too big for the Service Committee. They counselled that we should say no, with regrets. Then the chairman called for a period of silence, prayer, meditation. Ten or fifteen minutes went by in which no one spoke. The chairman opened the discussion once again. The view around the table was completely changed: "Of course, we have to do it." There was complete unity.

Truly worshipful decisions tend to occur in situations of high risk. Two examples would be the American Friends Service Committee's decision to send medical supplies to North Vietnam without a license and moments of high internal conflict such as the 1971 session of Philadelphia Yearly Meeting when Black militants seized the meeting house and demanded reparations. In neither of these cases was dramatic change of group opinion the outcome, although in the latter instance the initial anger among the assembled Friends was transformed under the leadership of the clerk of Yearly Meeting into patient worship. Faced with hundreds of silent worshippers, the militants soon gave up their angry harangues, asked the clerk's advice about how to proceed, and then invited the clerk to join their leader in chairing the meeting. Shortly thereafter, the militants withdrew and those Friends favoring reparations and those opposed were then able to agree to initiate an investment fund which would underwrite Black business enterprises.

The occasions when such dramatic religious depth is called for are not common. This writer observed situations approaching such depth three or four times in a year of attending Quaker meetings for business. In any matter of sufficient gravity that a Friend would be unwilling to step aside and let the group proceed, however, recourse is had to this explicitly religious level. The typical meeting oscillates between a superficial and a rather profound religious tone depending upon the topic under discussion.

In large measure, this oscillation is understandable. Only topics of import merit the high seriousness of a religious level of reflection. There would be something incongruous about deeply religious consideration of whether to have the meeting's mail delivered to the clerk's home or the caretaker's mailbox.[28] As one Friend put it, "If you try to go to the religious level all the time, you tend to strip that level of its meaning."

One obvious significance of decisions at the religious level is that they tend to draw greater acceptance from those present. One Friend spoke for many: "If the group seemed moved to its conclustion, yes, I'd feel much obligation. If the group didn't seem moved, then I'd feel less obligation." Similarly, Friends who feel opposed to a proposal on rational grounds tend to dismiss their opposition when they are aware of a religious quality to the tide (ancient Friends called it the current of Life)[29] they sense flowing in the opposite direction.

Belief that a decision is made under such divine auspices enlarges, as well, the type of decision the group is capable of making. One Friend commented: "Decisions based on human considerations are fine, but they're not enough for sacrifices of really important things like family and friends and life goals. When the North Carolina Quakers pulled up stakes and moved to Iowa because they felt drawn to dissociate themselves from a context of slavery, they were convinced it was a divine summons. Nothing else would have been enough to make them go."

Conflicting Myths and Fundamental Cleavages

The interviewer was surprised, however, by the large number of Quakers who do not seem to link the gathered situation of the meeting for worship with meeting for business at all. Time and again, there would be polite explanation that "gathered" or "covered" or "in the life" were synonymous terms referring to the sense of presence and unity of the meeting for worship, not the meeting for business. When pushed, these Friends would acknowledge that "something like that" did occasionally happen at meeting for business but that they had never thought it appropriate to use such language for the business context. Such respondents

84

typically tended to lean towards the universalist-humanist end of the religious spectrum, or to be devotees of the democratic or social activist myths.

Further questions sometimes led to the paradoxical discovery that, for some of these Friends, the experience of being gathered even in meeting for worship was more of a formal rather than an experiential reality. For some, the fact that the group had sat quietly for twenty-five minutes was itself identified as being gathered. For others, the meeting was gathered if the remarks by Friends in the closing minutes of the meeting were insightful. Along this same line, one helpful subject who agreed that meeting for business could be as gathered as meeting for worship indicated: "You can always tell whether a decision was taken in a gathered condition. Just look at the minute. If it's noted that a pause for reflection was made, the meeting was gathered." For these Friends, the gathered or covered meeting, where the community feels drawn into the Life and inspired by the Spirit, seems to be defined by externals. The American Friends Service Committee's decision to send penicillin to the National Liberation Front was remembered by one participant as not operative on the religious level because there was no official call for silence. Others described the same gathering as deeply in the Life: "No, there was not a lot of pausing for prayer. But you could sense a general feeling of the need of divine guidance. It showed in the remarks of some, the tone, the allusion to the Friends' ways of acting, to a lot of history that long predates the American Friends Service Committee."

If the latter speaker reflected the views of most of those present, still the puzzling difference in perceptions on this occasion seemed compounded as the researcher attempted to discuss with Friends their individual understandings of the religious significance of Quaker decisions. He soon found himself enmeshed in a world where everybody seemed to use the same vocabulary but with different meanings. For a moment it appeared that Lewis Carroll's Humpty Dumpty was hiding in each one: "When I use a word, . . . it means just what I choose it to mean—neither more nor less."[30]

If the researcher was to succumb to the all too typical canons of social science, he would probably scratch his head a few times at just this point, note that the ambiguity of Quaker expression makes accurate statistical evaluation of Quaker beliefs almost impossible without investment of untold time and effort, and move on to analysis of some less interesting but more manageable object of study.

It is true, after all, that Friends language is ambiguous. Moreover, the understanding of many Quakers in what they believe seems to shift according to the occasion or to be more inconsistent than they realize. The conflict between democratic equality and the theory that God's voice, not the weight of numbers, is to be followed by the meeting is just one clear example.

But to move on to other matters more conducive to measurement is to allow the limits of one's technology to control one's goals. In the best mystery stories of one's youth, the hidden treasure was usually found in a dimly lit room. So, too, the things most worth knowing are sometimes beyond the bright but short-range lights of social science research methodology.

In spite of preceding paragraphs, there is at least one major conclusion suggested by our research in this area. For in the midst of all the ambiguity involved in Quaker explanations of how their beliefs in a God, in social activism, and in democracy influence their decisions, the general pattern of their responses suggest a point which may be highly significant.

When Friends reflect upon their beliefs, they often focus upon the obvious conflict between Christocentric and universalist approaches.[31] People who feel strongly drawn to either camp often see the other position as a threat to Quakerism itself. Universalists dismiss Christocentrics as fundamentalists. Christocentrics suggest that the universalists have lost touch with the roots of Quakerism by abandoning the centrality of Christ which so influenced George Fox's philosophy.

For the devotee of either position, the first response to the interviewer tends to be that Quakerism has no formal doctrines and therefore the two groups live in harmony. When the conversation has gotten beyond such "official" responses, many a Friend has intimated at being ill-at-ease with the other group. When a Christocentric Friend stood at the 1975 Yearly Meeting to proclaim, "I consider all of you my Friends, but many I cannot consider my coreligionists,"[32] his remark was generally greeted with shocked dismay. But those individuals this reporter interviewed combined concern over the inappropriateness of the remark with acknowledgement that the point could not be ignored.

It would appear, in short, that the cleavage is between Christocentric and universalist Friends.

After most interviews were completed, this reporter began to feel uneasy with this understanding. True, Friends themselves are quite concerned over the dichotomy. True, such a basic conflict in beliefs is a plausible explanation for such Quaker difficulties as lack of growth and inability to hold new members. But, when the reporter reflected on the atmosphere and the tone of his interviews instead of the words that were exchanged, he began to find that the Christocentrics and certain universalists shared a sort of profound reverence for the gathered meeting for worship which was not readily found among other Friends.

When asked what they treasured most about Friends, Christocentrics and some universalists would typically recall a meeting for worship conducted in the Light. If asked to recall the business meeting decision that meant the most to them, they would often describe how some incident led the group to a gathered condition. Their words to explain the experience varied markedly, of course, but for both groups, the experience itself was what counted.

Asked the same questions, other universalists and Friends favoring what we have called the social action and the democratic myths might recall the same decision at a meeting for business or express their pride in a decision well made, but would be apparently unaware of the special atmosphere experienced by the others. Even when told directly that others in attendance reported a special sense of being gathered, such individuals were likely to comment, "That sort of thing doesn't much impress me," or "Other people can talk about their experience; I can only talk of mine."

Put simply, the real cleavage among Friends is between those who experience the gathered or covered condition and those who do not. The former can differ markedly in the language they use to verbalize the event. For one, the group is gathered in Christ; for the other, the force at the root of the universe or in the depth of every human is expressing itself in the covered assemblage. In either case, the words and concepts are secondary; the event, the experience, is what counts.

Between Friends who experience the covered condition and Friends who do not, there may be little difference in language. Universalist humanism, for example, may be intellectually satisfying to both. But the universalist humanism of the person who experiences the covered condition will lead in a quite different direction from the individual who does not have this experience. In the experience, the former finds guidance, motivation to reconsider preferences, a sense of obligation to the decision reached in this special atmosphere. None of these factors directly affects the person who has identical belief but lacks the experience. In this very important sense, those who share the experience, be they Christocentric or universalist or whatever else, are the coreligionists. Those who share intellectual understandings but do not share the experience are hardly co-religionists at all.

If this reporter's judgment of the cleavage point is accurate, then another factor demands consideration. Time and again older Friends would comment that the covered meeting is less common today than it was in their youth. To some extent, this recollection can be dismissed as a tendency towards nostalgia or as the memory's trick of recalling only the highlights of the past. Comparison of contemporary experience to a few Quaker journals from years gone by, however, suggests the decline is not merely a matter of faulty memory.[33]

One learned Friend remarked that the covered meeting is no rarer than the occasional sense of awe experienced at the most reverent moments of the Catholic Eucharist. Catholics, however, consider that the event of the Eucharist occurs whether the participants experience a sense of divine presence or not. The rarity of such an experience for Catholics, then, is not of central significance. Among Friends, where the experience has so much centrality that expressions of belief are incidental, the community that rarely prays in the Life has much more to fear.

It is very difficult to be accurate in discussing the frequency of covered meetings for worship. On a given occasion, the researcher may simply have been out of touch with the experience of the bulk of the community with which he was sharing worship. In checking his experience against that of others present, he may have picked those few who were as inattentive as he that morning. Or perhaps he simply frequented the wrong meetings for worship and business. (Of the ninety-nine monthly meetings in Philadelphia Yearly Meeting, only about ten were visited by the writer and some of these were visited only once.) For all that, it seems safe to say, on the basis of interviews and personal experience, that the great majority of worship sessions in the Yearly Meeting do not reach the gathered condition.

If this is so, could it be that the inclusion in the community of many who seem never to experience the gathered state is part of the reason why it is difficult for the community to achieve that condition? A racing shell wins few races if half its crew is not interested in manning the oars.

The irony of such a situation is that the very rarity of gathered meetings prevents those who are not oriented to such an experience from recognizing the significance of what they are missing. Said one Friend: "Why make such a big thing out of this gathered meeting business? That's surely not what attracted me to Quakerism, and Quakers get along by and large without it."

As if in reply, a longtime Friend remarked:

We have gotten lots of new members, especially in recent years, who are attracted by our testimonies—peace, racial harmony, women's rights, and the like. But it seems to me that most of these people will eventually leave us unless they become turned on by our worship. If they don't find something very special there, they will become impatient because we aren't so single-minded about such causes as they are. They'll tire of our slowness and they'll leave. After all, we try to base our actions on divine leadings. And that means we're more interested in finding the divine than in any given cause taken by itself.

It would be sad indeed if Friends who share the same experience but describe it in conflicting ways were to see each other as more divided by their language than united by their being gathered. So, too, it would be unfortunate if Friends who happen to share the same God-talk but who differ over the experience were to think that—in their religious heritage—the language is more uniting than the experience.

Chapter V

Quaker Leadership

Now that our essay has established that individuals and even groups are quite capable of group-centered action and has sketched the myths that support such a liberated action, it seems appropriate to explore the high expectations Quakers have for their leaders. We shall focus upon the one major official of Friends business meetings, the clerk.

The Clerk's Responsibilities: Devices for Hidden Control

Douglas Steere defines the clerk as a person whose personal belief in Quaker presuppositions expresses itself in some special qualities:

> He or she is a good listener, has a clear mind that can handle issues, has the gift of preparing a written minute that can succinctly sum up the sense of the meeting, and is one who has faith in the presuppositions that were mentioned earlier: faith in the presence of a Guide; faith in the deep revelatory genius of such a meeting to arrive at a decision that may break new ground and yet may in fresh ways be in keeping with the Society of Friends' deepest testimonies; and faith in each of those present being potentially the vehicle of the fresh resolving insight. With all of this, a good clerk is a person who refuses to be hurried and can weary out dissension with a patience borne of the confidence that there is a way through, although the group may have to return again and again to the issue before clearness comes and a proper decision is reached.[1]

Let us look at some of the clerk's ordinary duties and discover how they may also become levers of power.

Agenda

On the face of it, the clerk's responsibilities are extensive. The clerk prepares the agenda in advance. Although as one clerk put it, "they [clerks] consult others if they have sense,"[2] the final agenda is generally left to their judgment. The clerk's sense of the group may suggest ordering items so that the assembly will not be tired out before considering an issue of import, with less important matters saved until the end so that they can be dealt with quickly and efficiently. Or, the clerk may order agenda items so that an important topic upon which the group is likely to reach easy agreement comes early in the meeting and establishes a sense of confidence for dealing with a more difficult matter later in the session.

Stating the Questions and General Neutrality

Clerks will often be charged with summarizing a problem or framing a question as prelude to discussion. They are trusted to outline the facts and sketch two or three courses of action. They are expected to "be chary . . . of making known their own views" either initially or as discussion progresses.[3] Says one Friend, because the clerk's role is to "point the mirror [of the meeting] towards the Truth, he cannot try to be the source of the light."[4] This rule of neutrality is sometimes waived in very small, intimate monthly meetings, but not in major matters.

Evoking Comments from the Silent

The clerk must be especially alert to silent Friends. One clerk comments: "The clerk definitely should draw out those ill at ease. Even if you suspect some are opposed because of their silence, you should make them know their opinion is needed by the group." Another clerk tried to "draw out the shy people" by calling on every speaker by name.

Particularly in cases of hidden opposition, the clerk's action is important to the sense of obligation which the decision is likely to bring: "The clerk's big job is to look for the people who might remain silent now but will erupt after the decision is taken and the session has ended." The Friend whose silence allows him or her to withdraw feels less obligation to support the decision than the Friend who spoke against the proposal but finally chose to step aside. Because this individual participated and chose not to stand in the way, the vocal Quaker speaks of being obliged to go along. The individual who chose not to speak at the meeting may later talk after the event as if he or she had not been present, had no voice, and therefore has no part in what "they" did.

The positive side of this same phenomenon is the clerk's ability to build support for major decisions by polling the participants. An example of this would be the manner in which a new executive director was selected at Pendle Hill. After favorable discussion, the board chairman announced that the sense of the meeting favored the hiring of a particular individual. No one demurred. Then the clerk took the unusual step of going round the room and asking each of the sixty board members if they approved the action. Each responded affirmatively. The drama of the individual assents heightened the awareness that each board member supported the decision. Board members the writer spoke with later indicated a special sense of obligation to aid the new executive director.

Discipline

It is usually the clerk's responsibility to maintain discipline among the speakers. The long-winded speaker may find the clerk intervening to remark, "I think we've heard thy message." In recent years, the clerk of Philadelphia's Representative Meeting took a leaf from London Yearly Meeting's custom book. If a Friend was speaking too long, the clerk stood to signal that it was time to stop. In London, at least, this movement is so much a part of Friends practice that the offender who continues after the clerk rises is likely to hear, "the clerk is standing." Such a remark is ignored at one's peril.

At times the clerk's personal standing is so highly regarded that such disciplinary powers give great control over the proceedings. One participant in decisions at a Quaker college recalled, "If X was in the clerk's chair and looked unhappy or suggested that the point had already been made, the offender felt chastened." Such dominance is, in the writer's experience, rare.

Diplomacy and "Acting for the Uncomfortable Meeting"

The clerk's skills as a diplomat are also relied upon on occasion. "Chronic objectors must be dealt with considerately, even though their opinions may carry little weight."[5] The writer came across one decision in which a generally respected Friend seemed to object to every proposal on a particular topic. The committee was generally stymied. After a few weeks, the regular clerk returned from a trip and replaced his temporary substitute. In the next meetings, the objector's unhappiness was considered, but without the concern previously accorded it. The group moved forward quickly. Although the point was never discussed in the meetings of the committee, the members were aware that that objector's disagreement stemmed from a pet proposal the committee had decided against.

Said one participant, "The assistant clerk was just not up to coping with X." Clearly, Friends expect much of their clerks. A clerk remarked: "When faced with the chronic objector, the clerk must be gracious but firm. In a way, the clerk is always in a bind between reverencing the objector's opinion and acting for the uncomfortable meeting."

Clerks differ over the extent to which they believe they should utilize this power with which they are both entrusted and burdened. One respected clerk suggested that, as a last resort, clerks should do what they can to let the objector feel the weight of the meeting against the individual to make him or her feel isolated. Others disagreed strongly: "The objector is a child of God. Maybe in secular meetings you can operate this way. It just doesn't fit Friends' basic view of man." What impressed this observer was how consistently the latter view prevailed.

Judging What Is Important

Some clerks fear squelching any dissenter: "X sees the clerk as a servant who listens and records. He lets us go on and on. We can never finish anything on time." Other clerks are much more aggressive. One, commenting on Yearly Meeting sessions remarked: "I feel that if we delay a decision because we haven't complete clarity, if we let it run over into next year's meeting, we lose momentum, start next time from scratch and end up quitting again just where we left off the previous year."

We have already observed how this pressure to conclude discussion can bring unfortunate results when the sense of the meeting is announced before objectors have felt ready to withdraw their opposition. This is usually more a problem of finding a way to invite withdrawal than of anything more serious. However rare, real abuse of power can occur as well. The schism of 1827 was partly occasioned by a clerk of Yearly Meeting who called on Philadelphia Quaker businessmen far more frequently than Friends from farm country because he felt the businessmen had more significant things to say. Or more recently, a few years ago the clerk of one monthly meeting apparently just did not like a highly respected Friend. The clerk used his authority to weaken that Friend's positions by not calling on him, passing by his suggestions, etc. If the observer is struck by how rarely this sort of thing occurs, he also quickly realizes that the amount of judgment allowed the clerk makes such abuses possible.

Another sign of this same power is the reply we often received to questions about how a clerk ought to proceed if there is clearly a united meeting with the exception of one or two people who refused to stand aside for reasons the clerk has judged insignificant. One clerk spoke for many: "It happens fairly often. If the time is available, hold it over. If an immediate decision is needed, then I, as clerk, would ask, 'May we record your objection and proceed?' If the person is in his right mind, he'll say yes. If he is just plain unreasonable, then you make up your mind according to the factors in that individual case."

The writer has observed this sort of acquiescence by individuals to the plea of the clerk. Although the interchange was delicately polite, it seemed to boil down to a judgment by the clerk that the objector really ought to stand aside. The objector's acquiescence seemed to involve acceptance of the clerk's objectivity of judgment, a willingness to trust the esteemed and dispassionate observer.

Judging the Sense of the Meeting

The most important duty of the clerk is the clerk's responsibility to judge the sense of the meeting. One aspect of that judgment, as defined by Howard Brinton, is that "in gathering the sense of the meeting the clerk must take into consideration that some Friends have more wisdom and experience than others and their conviction should therefore carry greater weight."[6]

In practice, this means that a judgment must sometimes be made by the clerk about whether the support for a proposal constitutes a valid sense of the meeting, or instead, that the weight of the meeting is divided. Suppose fifteen people have spoken in favor of a proposal and three have spoken against it. Forty more Friends have not spoken more than an occasional "I agree" following one or other of a speaker's points. In trying to judge the sense of the meeting, the clerk is likely to consider the general reputation of the leading speakers for each viewpoint, the extent of information and experience each brings to the topic, the apparent conviction beneath a remark, and other intangible factors.

Just as difficult, the clerk must also assess the silent forty. Which of them are likely to have opinions on the matter? Are any of these likely to be opposed but silent? If so, it will probably be important to draw them into the discussion.

Such assessments by the clerk will determine whether the clerk feels there is a general trend in favor of the proposal or whether the discussion should continue. If the clerk feels there is a sense of the meeting, the clerk will probably propose a minute because further discussion would add nothing. On the other hand, the clerk may feel that the trend in favor of the proposal may not be completely reliable, perhaps because a few Friends whose opinions have not yet been heard may sway others. In this situation, it is better to delay offering a minute until the clerk is confident that these silent individuals do not in fact wish to speak.

The opportunity to manipulate is obvious. Suppose a clerk personally favors a proposal. A favorable early trend in discussion might provide the opportunity for the clerk to announce the sense of the meeting before opposed members have had a chance to speak. Such a premature announcement may lead to manipulation, especially if individual participants do not know that others share their misgivings. Instead, they may choose not to challenge the proposed minute, judging instead that: "I must be the only one who feels this way. I guess I won't bother to speak in opposition."

Again, since it is the clerk's normal task to propose a minute which expresses the sense of the meeting, one obvious way a clerk might influence an outcome is to slant the minute towards the position the clerk personally favors. Friends have developed protection against this weakness by urging that clerks take the time to propose their precise minute immediately at the end of discussion rather than to frame the minute vaguely and then wait until after the meeting has adjourned to express the decision exactly. London Yearly Meeting's book of discipline notes that different people are present from meeting to meeting so that a second meeting is often not in a position to challenge effectively the clerk's faulty summary of the sense of the first meeting.[7]

There are, of course, ways that the clerk can be kept honest. One Friend, asked how he would react to a clerk's framing a misleading minute, volunteered that he would withdraw confidence from the clerk and propose his own minute. A clerk, interviewed just after a meeting session commented:

> There's no way to make sure the clerk does everything perfectly. The behavior of the members can readily act as control on the clerk, however. If someone of some significance mentions from the floor that he doubts the minute was correct, the clerk may have reason to take this as a warning shot across the bow! If things are wandering, someone from the floor can encourage the clerk to give direction by asking the clerk to suggest a minute. Today that happened to me. At the meeting just concluded, others' questions obliged me as clerk to offer tentative minutes.

Superficially, the clerk can be seen as a Quaker equivalent of the Speaker of the House of Commons: by the very structure of British parliamentarism, the Speaker is an impartial servant of the House. The

Speaker's responsibility to remain unbiased is enforced by the ability of the parties to expose any inappropriate actions the Speaker might take. In the Quaker case, however, the rules by which the meeting proceeds are much more informal, so that only gross violations of equity can be challenged. And the areas in which the clerk is expected to exercise judgment, especially the central responsibility of declaring the sense of the meeting, are far broader than the circumscribed powers allowed the Speaker.

Self-Restraint

The clerk, then, is entrusted with an unusual amount of authority. Although there are some checks on that authority, they are not especially forceful so long as a clerk is circumspect in his or her manipulative efforts. If the formal constraints are minimal, however, contemporary abuse of power seems curiously rare.

One cannot help being struck by the trust in the integrity of the clerk which is typical of Quaker meetings, a trust so complete that clerks speak with reverence of the duty the community asks them to perform. This simple trust came home to the writer most forcefully one evening when a woman commented as she exited the meeting room, "I really thought the sense of the meeting was something completely different until the clerk voiced it." Clearly the woman so trusted the clerk's judgment that she put aside her own evaluation without hesitation. The observer, who also had read a different sense of the meeting from that of the clerk, wondered how many others in the room had cheerfully substituted the clerk's evaluation for their own.

In a similar vein, the observer was struck by the frequent cases in which—in spite of the wise advice that the clerk should present a full minute for approval at the session—meetings would cheerfully trust the clerk to write a minute after the meeting which reflected the nuances of their agreement. Part of this was practical haste to cover the agenda by not wasting time over trifles like the proper sequence of names on a flyer. Sometimes the matter was of more consequence, as when a monthly meeting drew up guidelines for sensitively contacting lapsed members prior to dropping them from membership.[8] Especially in the more important matters, such trust indicated the meeting's confidence in the clerk.

To the observer, this attitude seems truly justified. One cannot help noticing the scrupulous efforts of a typical clerk to draw into the discussion any individuals who might help to bring clarity to an important issue.

A clerk who is unsure of the discussion's trend will ask for help from the floor. Such conduct is hardly suggestive of a desire to manipulate the deliberations.

When this reporter interviewed Friends of long experience, he found that they talked freely of situations a generation or two back when individual clerks controlled their meetings. But they contrasted such control to the present situation.

The great caution clerks feel about abuse of power came out frequently in interviews. One respected clerk mentioned that sometimes a clerk frames a "false" minute in hopes of alerting the meeting to the drift of its discussion and jolting the participants in the process. If a meeting is discussing civil rights and begins to trade stories of imprudent use of Quaker seed money by certain black entrepreneurs, the clerk might suggest, "Friends seem to feel that this fund has been ill-used and should therefore be discontinued." The impact of the tentative minute, much akin to summary statements by the therapist in nondirective counselling, may serve to force the group to face its attitudes squarely.

When asked whether this approach would be legitimate, clerks were of divided opinion. One group objected to the strategy because the clerk's position was too central to the meeting to permit proposing such a false minute. For these clerks, any such conduct was dangerous manipulation which, if recognized, ought to deprive the clerk of the respect of the group.

Another group considered the advice legitimate but dangerous: "There's a great tendency in our system to accept what the clerk offers. The suppositions all go with the clerk. The false minute approach is too subtle, [and it] may just stampede the meeting down a false road."

Both groups revealed in their reluctance an impressive sensitivity to the clerk's possible abuse of power. This sensitivity appeared again and again in their interview comments, with the most experienced clerks appearing most chary of abuse. One suspects that such is the case partly because the experienced clerk has had more opportunity to observe the ramifications of even the slightest excess in fulfilling the office and partly because longevity in clerking implies that the individual has been asked time and again to assume this office by nominating committees and constituencies that are especially attentive to the person's past record of honest impartiality.

If one adds to these factors the frequency with which clerks describe their role in explicitly religious terms—clerks seem much more comfortable with the religious implications of Friends decision making than did nonclerks—one rounds out the factors which are most prominent in the self-restraint clerks seem to exercise. The "faith in the presence of a Guide [and] in the deep revelatory genius of [the] meeting" which Douglas Steere outlined in the first citation in this chapter is typical of a clerk's remarks. Since the clerk is, of all the participants, the person most fully responsible for finding the unity in which the Guide is revealed, it is not surprising that the clerk's commitment to this fundamental Quaker belief tends to be a powerful protection against temptations to indulge a desire to control the outcomes.

Quaker Leadership: Ability to Read

Leadership in the Religious Society of Friends demands the intertwining of traditional basic leadership skills with a peculiar skill at reading the sense of the meeting. The basis of this conclusion, and some of its implications, are explored below.

Management Types

In his now classic analysis, Douglas M. McGregor divides conceptions of management's task into two widely accepted categories. The "theory X" manager believes that he is responsible for modifying the behavior of his naturally indolent, self-centered, gullible, and irresponsible subordinates so that their behavior fits the needs of the organization. Whether his style is harsh or gentle, his suppositions remain the same.[9]

In contrast, the "theory Y" manager believes that his subordinates are concerned about organizational needs, capable of assuming responsibility, and naturally well-motivated. The manager's task is to provide conditions that promote the use of the potential in the people of the organization. The wise manager realizes that the psychologist, Abraham Maslow's hierarchy of emergent needs must be honored: it is not enough to satisfy physiological and safety needs, for these are only prelude to the higher human needs the motivated employee will seek to fulfill through his role in the organization.[10]

On its face, the theory X approach is inconsistent with Quaker decision making because it places responsibility on the manager and Friends decisions are supposed to emerge from the group. This is not to say, however, that there are no theory X managers in the Religious Society of Friends. Admittedly, such individuals seem rare among clerks of monthly and higher level meetings. But they do tend to emerge in other roles in which their expertise makes their "recommendations" unchallengeable by the meeting. One such person made herself the unsurpassed expert on the history of her meeting's burial ground. Another, his meeting's treasurer, made the books so complicated that only he could divine their true meaning. Occasionally, staff employees of Philadelphia Yearly Meeting have been known to adopt a similar tack in submitting proposals to supervising bodies whose judgment they did not regard highly. Such individuals attempt to parlay their exclusive expertise into control over decisions touching their specialty.

It would seem that their style imposes a fundamental limitation on these people. Although "horror stories" of previous generations suggest that such individuals did at times become clerks of meetings, the general abhorrence for such domination in the present day seems to explain why the upward mobility of the theory X manager is thwarted today.

The theory Y approach to management is more congenial to Friends practice, for it presumes that all the subordinates will be participants in the shaping of policy. Of fundamental import, however, is the reality that Quaker theory sees the clerk or other leader as servant of the meeting, not its director. The clerk does not collect ideas, then make a decision which incorporates as far as possible the group's contributions. Although things may sometimes work in just that way, the clerk's true role is to articulate the unity which he or she discovers in the community and to facilitate the formation of that unity. But the clerk is not to make the decision unilaterally.[11]

The Quaker leader, then, is not a practitioner of theory X. In the role of clerk, he or she feels comfortable with the focus on the group of theory Y, but not with its expectation that the leader is the decision maker. If we are to come to real understanding of leadership as it occurs in the Religious Society of Friends, we must move beyond these normal management categories.

Beyond Type Y: The Leader As Reader

When one questions experienced clerks and other seasoned Friends about the special qualities they would like to see in a clerk, one finds a great unity in their answers. One individual speaks of "artistry" in the "ability to sense the right timing for a given group." Others remark upon the clerk's "special gift" of sensing when the decision has been reached. This "true gift" is so reliable that "the good clerk knows whether people are saying what they really think."

It is interesting to see how often Friends resort to the language of "gift" in describing the skill of the clerk. A listener with even minimal acquaintance with traditional theological language is struck by the similarity between what Quakers report they find in their best clerks and the New Testament notion of the charisma or gratuitous gift given a believer to facilitate the public life of the Church. Among the predominant forms of charismata in the ancient Church were listed wisdom, knowledge, discernment of inner spiritual motions in oneself and in others, and gifts of government.[12] We discussed in Part One the gift of discernment which George Fox claimed. It would appear that, although modern Friends may be unaware of the theological language, their experience points them to the event that language describes. For our own purpose, in place of the theological language of charismata we will be content to refer to the phenomenon as the ability to "read" the group.

We have already given enough examples of this ability to read the unity of the group to illustrate the clerk's role. Since this ability is not automatically limited to those who are clerks, perhaps an example or two of nonclerks exercising this sort of leadership would be helpful. One clerk, when asked whether she sometimes erred in judging the sense of the meeting, replied: "Every once in a while you get called fairly on a minute. I remember once a discussion on whether to buy a bookkeeping machine. I declared that Friends didn't seem to have reached unity and therefore the decision must be delayed. Then X rose and suggested that Friends were really quite ready to buy the machine. This drew general approval. He had just read the feeling of the meeting better than I."

The decision described above fits the pattern of a number we have observed, and the dynamic is worthy of note. When the clerk announced that there had appeared to be no unity, the bulk of the participants probably accepted her reading of the situation without challenge. People who knew they themselves approved the purchase did not question the clerk's judgment that approval was not universal. Only the man with the ability to read the group well was ready to suggest that the clerk's reading had been faulty: hesitancy expressed in previous speakers' remarks was not as deep-seated as she had thought. The test of his assessment, of course, was the immediate response of the individual members of the meeting. Anyone who personally was unwilling to proceed with the purchase could have stood and said so, and in that case, the clerk's reading would have been confirmed.

Here is another example which combines ability to read a group with the respect the group accords an individual blessed with the ability of reading deeply. In November 1970, a special committee called "The 1970

Working Party" reported to Philadelphia Representative Meeting its proposals for self-examination as a tool to discovering racism within the Yearly Meeting. The Working Party asked authorization to contact all members of the Yearly Meeting and all Yearly Meeting organizations in order to ask that Friends look "to their possessions, practices, and relationships 'to try whether the seeds' of exploitation and oppression lie in them."[13] Discussion was lively and much divided. Many felt comfortable with the proposal; many others saw in it a document which could alienate Friends or which falsely presumed that racism was deeply rooted with the Yearly Meeting. Some feared that such self-examination was intended as a prelude to a call for reparations to the black community. The issue so divided those present that they agreed the next month's session would convene early to allow for an hour's silent worship to let everyone think the document through deeply and, it was hoped, find unity in the shared silence of the worship. In the interim, of course, the Working Party's proposal would not be sent out.

The next month's session occurred as agreed. Silent worship was interspersed with a few deeply-felt messages from individual worshipers who spoke of their concerns on both sides of the issue. In the business session which followed, the participants were asked to try to maintain the spirit of worship as they discussed the issue. At this point, it was not at all clear that unity would likely be reached. The clerk remarked that she saw no agreement.

At this juncture, a Friend known for his ability to read the community stood to speak. He had been silent in the previous month's discussion and was not predictably of either party in the present disagreement. He remarked simply that, for the last month, he had kept the proposal of the Working Party on the nightstand next to his bed along with his volume of the traditional testimonies and concerns of the Religious Society of Friends. He had read the Working Party's document many times. He was satisfied that not one word of it was in conflict with the traditions of Friends.

The whole discussion changed. People who had been opposed spoke of how to temper any possible misunderstandings of the proposal. Attention focused on how best to present the document so that it would have fullest effect. The Working Party's proposal was approved and forwarded to the monthly meetings.[14]

Almost five years later, the writer interviewed the Friend whose remarks had been so significant in the decision. Early in the discussion, he seemed ill at ease, even suspicious of what underlay the interviewer's interest. But when the incident in question was mentioned, his tone changed entirely to one of serious reverence. In reflecting on the event he remarked:

> Sometimes there is not the time for a large number to speak, and slowly, slowly for an acceptable solution to emerge. Or perhaps there is no desire by many to speak even though they are not satisfied with the proposal on the floor.
>
> So we need leadership. It seems contrary to Friends theory, doesn't it? Perhaps it's a weakness, given our theory, that leadership is still needed. Within our groups, certain people will be followed when they speak. Typically, there's lots of discussion until one person—often a person with skill at doing it, skill that's soon recognized by the group and expected to emerge at critical times—stands up and proposes what all can buy. The great arguer isn't this sort of person. It's not that type of leadership. Personally, I try to see both sides, make myself keep quiet until I understand the whole question. And then, sometimes, I feel moved to speak.

The case illustrates a number of factors common to this sort of situation. The group feared disunity, and was attempting to conduct itself in a prayerful, even a gathered atmosphere. The speaker himself felt moved to speak. The speaker's remarks were so deeply consistent with the atmosphere of united, reverent searching that he seemed to speak in a divinely authenticated way.[15]

Here, then, is a combination of ability to read the community's attitudes and to lead the community to a new unity. The speaker is doing two things at once. The two cannot be separated. Because he knows the extent of their unity of desire, he is able to call them to a unity of commitment to a course of action. The latter unity does not exist before he calls them. This ability to judge not only the unity that is real but also the unity that is now possible is in the deepest sense the charisma which marks Quaker leadership.

This is the quality that Friends look for when they are selecting clerks. It should be no surprise to the reader that the man who spoke up at the critical moment concerning the Working Party's proposal is the same person that suggested the clerk was in error about the business machine. A few years later he was selected to be clerk of the Yearly Meeting.

Some Weaknesses of Friends Leadership

Every machine breaks down. Every system of government has its flaws. The Quaker form of leadership provides a great support to the goal of reaching unity on divisive questions. But that form of leadership, too, has weaknesses.

Lack of Congruence Between Gifts

The most obvious problem is that there is no guarantee that individuals with the ability to read the community accurately will also excel in the basic organizational skills required for running a meeting. Nor are all those who know how to keep a meeting moving at an effective pace capable of reading the leanings of the members. Then again, there are some Friends able to read groups but not especially patient when asked to clerk a meeting. Some monthly meetings and other Quaker groups find themselves with clerks who are selected because of their strength in one area in spite of weakness in another. Where basic organizational skills are lacking, one notes severe disorganization of meetings. Where the clerk combines excellent perception of trends with impatience, one finds meetings which feel cowed by the dominance of the clerk who announces agreement before some participants are ready to acknowledge—even to themselves—that they have in fact changed their opinion. Given this spectrum of possible combinations of strengths and weaknesses, the visitor should not be too surprised to discover quite different styles and emphases in various Quaker groups using the same fundamental procedures.

Abdication of Responsibility by "Ungifted" Quakers

We have already mentioned the woman who thought the sense of the meeting was completely different until the clerk voiced it. Friends who are timid or hesitant to take stands will sometimes sit back and leave it to the clerk and other vocal leaders to thrash out the pros and cons of an issue and reach a conclusion. The display of special gifts by these leaders seems to provide a justification for the "ungifted" to refuse entry into the process. Although Quaker theory holds firmly that the community needs to hear that of God in every one, the presence of individuals of special skill seems to make it easier for more ordinary people to excuse themselves from participation. In conversations during coffee breaks and after meetings, this writer was often struck by the phenomenon of people who had remained silent but who now went out of their way to exclaim over how lucky the meeting was to have one of the more gifted vocal participants.

Overmuch Influence by the Readers at Critical Junctures

The sort of abuse we are about to discuss is one against which Quaker

104

method has little defense. We raise this point with some hesitancy. However, the abuse can be very significant. The efforts made by Quaker leaders to avoid abuse are impressive, yet their very sensitivity to the matter indicates how dangerous it can be. We refer to the ability of readers to use their special status in the community to lead the group to their personal preference under guise of identifying an as yet unrecognized area of unity.

The clerk or the nonclerk who has demonstrated the ability to read the meeting is accorded high regard because of his or her skill. Theologically, this role is heightened because Friends consider unity a sign of divine guidance. The individual who can discern the unity is thus a seer.

Such a person quickly exercises an influence that is subtle and pervasive. The supposed agreement that the reader enunciates—because the reader has enunciated it—has innate authority. Individuals in the group who had not thought of the position offered by the reader are highly receptive to it because, coming from this person, it probably is right for the group. Individuals explicitly opposed to the position tend to reconsider their position, sometimes squelching their doubts on the grounds that the gifted person probably is reading the group correctly even if their own reading of the group had been just the opposite.

Add to this the ordinary dynamic of group action that potential solutions are usually accepted more readily when the group has discussed long enough to feel frustration and to fear that no decision will be reached, and you suddenly discover that the theologically right moment to speak up is often the psychologically right moment. Thus, the person who comes to the meeting with a solution in his back pocket might wait until the group seems ripe for the idea instead of proposing it at the outset. In Quakerism, this ploy may become wrapped in the garb of inspiration as the group confuses the speaker's prepared in advance suggestion for an inspired reading of the present level of agreement of the assembly.

The writer recalls a casual conversation with a woman who sat next to him at a meeting for business. She mentioned what she thought would be the best approach to an issue dividing the community. The visitor asked whether she would suggest her solution as soon as the topic came to the floor. "No," she said, "I doubt they'd be ready for it. You have to wait for the right moment."

The topic was introduced. She waited. Discussion revealed the main pros and cons. She waited. Discussion became involved and repetitious. After about five more minutes, she stood to offer her solution. It was received with gratitude, discussed briefly, then approved.

This apparent manipulation is not a simple matter. Perhaps the woman in question had been thinking the matter through prayerfully and had felt led the day before to offer this solution. If so, should she have offered it at a psychologically inappropriate moment? Clearly, if her message was from the Lord, she was not given it for use at any moment except the one when it would do the most good.

Or perhaps she had no particular feeling that her solution was from the Lord. She still felt it was a good solution. Why shouldn't she wait until the time when the group would be most receptive?

Certainly, had she wrapped her suggestion in the trappings of revelation by calling for her listeners to center down, and appearing to speak out of her present religious leadings, she would have been guilty of manipulation. Since she did not do that, was it her fault that some in the community might take her suggestion as a reading of the group's hidden potential for unity when she was in fact only gauging whether the group was frustrated and confused enough to be ripe for her ready-made solution? Such a person has read the group's confusion, not its unity.

We do not wish to place overmuch emphasis upon this matter. Suffice it to say that Quaker suppositions can sometimes elevate a contribution that is merely a timely offering of a preset position into a spontaneous insight by a speaker. Thus, a tactical measure can be elevated to a religious revelation, and the individual reputed to be a reader holds dangerous power to sway the community.

The writer has been sure he was dealing with such a situation only on the one occasion already cited. At many another time, however, it struck this observer that the situation was ripe for such manipulation or that there was no conceivable way to determine whether a proposal of possible unity which the community then accepted was in fact the product of insight or of prior planning. It is good that Friends noted for the ability to read are so aware of the obligation they bear to self-discipline in use of their special gift. For the community has little defense against such a gift should it be carefully misused. Only the teetotaler is a safe guard for the liquor.

Conclusion

Conclusion

This conclusion explores three topics. First, a theme which emerged in the historical section but which was not a prime focus for the contemporary study is completed. Secondly, the writer attempts some unabashed speculation on the negative implications of American society for the future of Quakerism. And thirdly, reflection upon Quakerism's possible significance for the future of American society.

Completing a Theme: Local Autonomy Versus Central Hegemony Today

The historical chapters of this study traced out a surprising tendency for central control to supersede the sovereignty of the monthly meeting. This accretion was unexpected, given the core Quaker idea that divine guidance is found in the religious experience of the gathered local community. Our historical pages limited their attention to early growth in England. Are there any resonances of tension between local and central authority to be found in contemporary American Quakerism?

There are resonances. The best way to understand them is to recall that, unlike British Friends, American Quakers did not suffer widespread persecution in their early years. Hence, they felt little pressure to establish a superstructure as a defense against the government. The American version of London Meeting for Sufferings began only in the 1750s and never wielded the power of its much earlier British counterpart. There was no yearly meeting bureaucracy, no paid staff until well into the twentieth century.

Since the historical English pressures toward central leadership were lacking, the emergence of centripetal tendencies had to await the develop-

109

ment of the twentieth century yearly meeting bureaucracy. The greater efficiency and impact of central preparation of religious books and central coordination of social welfare programs and protest in contemporary American society has meant growth of the Philadelphia Yearly Meeting budget to something over one million dollars per year.[1] Friends with special interest in the matters covered by the Yearly Meeting budget gravitate towards yearly meeting committees and projects and spend proportionately less time on their own monthly meetings. This emphasis leads to cleavage. One Friend explains:

> Interest turns someone into what we call a "Yearly Meeting Friend."
> Volunteers and employees of Yearly Meeting tend, therefore, to be the
> most committed, the most "far out" on issues. Their commitment makes
> them strong on leadership. The real tension between their actions and
> the more conservative leanings of many monthly meetings, where less
> socially aware Friends tend to be found, comes to be a sore point.

In practice, complaints from monthly meetings often concentrate upon the autonomy of the Yearly Meeting staff and its apparent lack of sensitivity to the reluctance of monthly meetings to endorse its acts. Unhappy Friends also claim that the large Yearly Meeting budget for social welfare programs drains local money to the Yearly Meeting with the result that the local projects of monthly meetings are often overshadowed. (Those who are interested in social welfare matters often tend to follow the money to the Yearly Meeting where others of like conviction are already gathered.) One of the modes of making this local unhappiness felt is annual foot-dragging over increases in the Yearly Meeting budget.

As a balance to this dissatisfaction, even Friends who are saddened by expansion and tendencies of what they term the "Philadelphia Vatican" comment upon the value to all meetings of the central services provided. First Day school materials and media coverage of Friends public testimonies at the Yearly Meeting level are common instances of this counterweight.

Yearly Meeting leaders, sensitive to the delicacy of the balance, have made notable efforts to meet valid criticism by adjusting central procedures. Public actions by the spirited members of the Peace Committee have been kept under tighter rein in response to local criticisms. For example, letters of complaint to foreign heads of state must now be approved by Representative Meeting or its Executive Committee before they can be dispatched. Yearly Meeting staff members have become more alert to the need to prepare the way for programs they are interested in by visiting monthly meetings, informing them of their intended activities, and obtaining their blessing. However, in spite of many such efforts to temper central autonomy over the past ten years, unhappiness in monthly meetings continues to run deep.

In sum, the centrifugal genius of Quaker tradition is in tension with the centripetal force of central effectiveness. But the tension seems a healthy one which increases central accountability, expands communication, and keeps individual monthly meetings from gradually drifting into an isolation which could weaken the cohesion of the Religious Society of Friends. At least for the moment, there is a dynamic tension which bodes well for the Quaker future.

Speculation: The Future of Quakerism

A topic of serious concern among members of Philadelphia Yearly Meeting is the significant decline in the number of adult members. In the twenty years since 1960 to 1980, the community has lost adult members at a rather steady annual rate just under one-half percent a year—a decline of almost ten percent over twenty years. When Friends add to this decrease the problem that many of the present 11,000 adult members neither attend meeting for worship nor respond to monthly meeting requests for financial support, they become fearful that the Society of Friends in the Philadelphia region is in an unhealthy condition.[2] Friends wonder why.

Our visits to meeting for business at various monthly meetings frequently made us ask whether we had selected a bad night. Attendance of even 10 percent of the members of the meeting began to seem quite acceptable after a few such visits. A number of Friends volunteered that they were disturbed by the paucity of participants in local meetings for business. This attendance record contrasted vividly with that of Representative Meeting where at least 70 percent of the members could be relied upon to be present each month.

In reflecting on possible explanations for the contrasting attendance of these two groups, we found our thoughts moving paradoxically towards the great strengths of Quaker decision making. We have already noted that out of a united decision also comes a high degree of obligation to carry out the decision and make it work. Every participant either actively favored the proposal or, at least, could have stopped the action but did not. The price one pays for attending a meeting for business is that one leaves with new obligations. The individual cannot claim to be merely a disinterested observer.

If one adds to this obligation the presupposition in Quaker decisions that each participant is willing to start from the viewpoint of the group's

111

good and not from a personal perspective, one suddenly comes face-to-face with an even broader price demanded of the participant. Each person must make a fundamental shift from the atomic individuality which marks American society and embrace a communitarian starting point.

Could it not be that Quakerism is a victim of the general culture? People socialized into the atomism (or individualism) which has been fundamental to Western thought since the rise of liberalism need special abilities if they are successfully to shift into a subculture which expects a communitarian self-understanding. The Quaker who mistakenly reduces Friends decision making to democracy sees no advantage in the extra time taken by "quaint" procedures. "Why not just vote and get it over with?" is the sort of question sometimes asked. The individual who must ask this sort of question is approaching Quakerism from the outside, from a thought-world alien to its very foundations.

Such a person neither accepts the communitarian self-understanding nor the obligations which the decisions of the meeting for business place upon the individual. The best way to avoid the obligations is by avoiding the meetings. The absent Friend does not incur the burden of the Friend who is present and who therefore is personally responsible for the decision.

An individual opting for absence has plenty of support from social trends. Fewer Friends are self-employed and more women have full-time positions in the workforce in addition to family responsibilities. Families move frequently and tend to be less interested in any communities larger than their own family unit. In other words, the economic and social trends in our individual-centered society provide a constant, pervasive impetus towards thinking of a communitarian worldview as an impossible burden.

If our speculation is right, it explains why we found the Quaker business procedure so effectively utilized in most of the meetings we visited. Those in attendance were generally capable of entering the communitarian thought-world and accepting the obligations the meeting was to impose. Friends unable to shift into that world and to bear its burdens tended not to come. Put another way, one reason the Philadelphia Yearly Meeting faces declining membership statistics is that it is faithful to its heritage, a heritage that more and more of its members are incapable of sharing.

Such an explanation fits rather well with the responses we received in casual encounters with individuals who had given up their Quakerism. These people consistently spoke highly of the social testimonies of Friends

112

and of Quaker tolerance for diversity of belief within the community. But they revealed puzzlement, boredom, and irritation when the conversation turned to the "peculiar" Quaker approach to decision making.

Supposing for the moment that our analysis is correct, the avenues open to Friends are rather limited. First, they could take the tack followed by groups like the Old Colony Mennonites who, when their culture was being eroded by the world, required members to divorce themselves from contact with worldly life and to immerse themselves instead in the Mennonite community.[3] Given the Quaker genius for full involvement in American life, such a prospect of segregation seems out of the question.

A second approach might be to emphasize, in the education of both adult members and of the children of members, the possibility of "nonatomic" starting points for human life. Instead of focusing on themselves as individual atoms, as units basically separate from the world about them, Friends would be taught to see themselves fundamentally as participants in larger communities, and only secondarily as atomic individuals. Friends grammar and high schools, study groups, and First Day schools are all obvious places for explicitly exploring the implications for human life of a communitarian self-understanding. Surely a religious society which includes in its membership a notable percentage of people committed to counterculture lifestyles should find it easy to carry its critical analysis of American society to a level deep enough for the limitations of atomic self-understanding to be perceived. In contrast, the Quaker communitarian presuppositions might be offered as a sound alternative world view.

A third mode of confronting the problem might be to reemphasize the importance of religious experience in Quaker life. The gathered meeting for worship could be cultivated once again through special attention in Quaker magazines, more emphasis upon religious retreats where private and group worship might be deepened, and other attempts at consciousness raising.

Simultaneously, Friends charged with interviewing applicants for monthly meeting membership might become much more sensitive as to whether the candidate values the religious experience in Quaker life and can understand and rate highly the gathered condition of a meeting. All too often, such matters may be considered inappropriate areas for inquiry; and committees which screen applicants may content themselves with the assumption that the prospective Friend finds Quaker social testimony or fellowship attractive.

Similar questions might also be asked in making decisions about whether to retain inactive resident members on the rolls of the monthly meeting. Retaining as members virtually all who have not explicitly asked that their names be removed from the list—the practice of many monthly meetings—tends to reduce membership to a meaningless level; one can remain a Friend even if one's participation in the community's life is limited to occasional inquiries into the state of one's grandfather's grave. Honestly recognizing that such individuals are not full members might underscore the importance for Quaker life of the shared religious experience which gathers individual members beyond atomic existence into a unity. Once again, the experiential root of Quakerism might receive the prominence it deserves.

Speculation: Quakerism's Message for the American Future

A number of the writer's confreres in graduate school, upon hearing that this study dealt with Quaker decision making, presumed that he would find the Quaker process to be a variant on the unanimous consent of the United States Senate or the tendency of United Nations committee chairmen to declare that "there being no objection, the committee approves the following." Some Friends suggested the same conclusions, often pointing to the United Nations in particular as a secular example of Quaker method.

The author's research has convinced him that almost exactly the opposite is true. In the United States Senate, unanimous consent is typically a device for approving matters which arouse no one's opposition and is used as a method of expedition. Unanimity thus means that the matter is trivial or noncontroversial. The members of the Senate are not called upon to change from the atomic vantage point of their own and their constituents' interests to a community-based perspective. They simply affirm that the matter does not adversely affect their set of interests.

In the United Nations, unanimous consent is very frequently a way for nations to avoid going on record. By making arrangements behind the scenes, nations reach a compromise inconsistent with the official formulations of their individual foreign policies but seen as advantageous, here and now, to their national interests. By the subterfuge of failure to vote, they can preserve their officially formulated positions, yet serve their immediate national needs. Such a procedure may imitate some aspects of Quaker decision making, but it lacks both the change from national to community interest and the commitment to participate in achieving the

114

agreed goal which are central to the Friends process.[4]

Another area suggested from time to time as an instance of the Friends style of decision is the deliberations of the corporate board. Although we do not wish to argue that such instances never occur, we must suggest that many apparent similarities between the Quaker style of decision making and those of the board room are only coincidental. We recall a Friend who commented enthusiastically about a Philadelphia corporation he knew which reached unanimous decisions at its board meetings with only rare exceptions. However, another Friend, a member of a number of corporate boards, remarked:

> Sure, corporations' boards of directors almost always agree. That's just good business. You pick a management team and then you back them unanimously until some major segment of the board is dissatisfied enough to want to replace the team. Until you want to make that major change, you would only be weakening management unnecessarily by voting no or no confidence. So, when you vote yes, it has little in common with Quaker unity. This kind of yes just means you haven't enough votes to win yet.

In short, apparent parallels to Friends decision making seem to fall far short because they do not demand of the participant the characteristic Quaker change of viewpoint or burden the individual with the Quaker sense of obligation to make the decision work out successfully. In a fundamental sense, the supposed parallels differ from Friends decisions because the former do not presuppose that participants are in community.

Our speculation thus raises a fundamental issue. Individualized, atomic man cries out for community. He or she complains because of the inability to participate in a satisfying way in decision making that affects his or her life.[5] But individualized, atomic man is incapable of community because of the inability to surrender the individual-focused starting point which has been fundamental to Western culture since the beginning of liberalism.[6] Therefore all attempts by a person whose socialization has been locked into the atomic thought-world to achieve the community longed for are doomed to fail, doomed to imitate the externals of a participation based upon communion without ever quite attaining the communion itself that would transform those externals into reality.

Roberto Unger, Harvard political philosopher, argues forcefully that now is the time for a "total criticism," a critique of social theory which would not rest content to challenge parts of the present thought-world but would attempt to challenge that world's very roots. The outcome would

115

be a turning away from liberalism's atomic man so that tomorrow's man could once again escape the isolation of viewpoint basic to liberalism and find a fuller identity as part of an "organic group" whose good and goals would be the initial point of reference.[7] Tomorrow's world of thought would go beyond liberalism in order to embrace a new level of community.

Our speculation leaves both Quakerism and the American future in doubt. If the American society becomes even more deeply mired in an atomic world view, we can expect the number of people capable of living in both an American and a Quaker universe to diminish gradually and constantly. Eventually, this could spell the end to such Quaker units as Philadelphia Yearly Meeting.

On the other hand, if the hunger for community is strong and growing, might not the number of Americans who are ready for a group such as Friends be expected to increase? In that case, Friends would still face the great challenge of helping these people to enter the Quaker experience deeply enough to be able to change their basic thought-world from the atomic to the communitarian. But, if Friends are successful, groups like the Philadelphia Yearly Meeting might be the vanguard of a new revolution.

And so we conclude with Quakerism in an ambiguous state. Will the Religious Society of Friends become a victim of the atomic society or a beacon drawing that society to the community which its members crave?

Alfred North Whitehead remarks: "Profound flashes of insight remain ineffective for centuries, not because they are unknown, but by reason of dominant interests which inhibit reaction to that type of generality. The history of religion is the history of the countless generations required for interest to attach itself to profound ideas."[8]

Centuries ago, George Fox found on Pendle Hill an experience that spoke to his condition. Is it too much to suppose that modern seekers might find in the Religious Society of Friends the religious experience and worldview that would speak to theirs?

Appendix A
Appendix B
Notes
Bibliography

Appendix A

The Christian Tradition of Divine Guidance

Many a Quaker whom the author has interviewed during research for this book has suggested that the Friends decision process is something doubly miraculous; not only does it achieve harmony without resorting to voting, it was virtually revealed to George Fox and is unheard of elsewhere in the Christian tradition. The harmony derived from disparate opinions may indeed qualify at times for a miraculous label. However it is the purpose of this appendix to demonstrate that Friends decision making is not a process which abruptly began with the inspirations of George Fox but, instead, is an important example of a rich tradition which has marked the Christian community from the days of the Apostles and which especially flourished at the time Fox founded his movement.

Where, then, did early Quakers get their extraordinarily practical theology of divine guidance? One source is Scripture.

Acts 15 recounts a church council at Jerusalem in which it seemed good to the Apostles and the elders and with the whole church to send a letter to the Gentile Christians freeing them from the obligation of circumcision. The letter included the clause, "it has seemed good to the Holy Ghost, . . . and to us. . . ."[1] Robert Barclay's *Anarchy of the Ranters* focused on this episode to explain Quaker practice.[2]

Did George Fox simply read the Book of Acts, meditate on its implications, and create the Quaker process? Hardly. Fox's procedure was not nearly as singular in the mid-seventeenth century as it may seem in the late-twentieth. An overview of the precursors of the Quaker method will reveal the extent to which Quaker procedures were already in the air.

Medieval Catholic Practice

Medieval Catholic procedure is helpful for indicating how widespread was the expectation that the Holy Spirit would be active in directing the outcome of ecclesiastical decision making. For example, bishops were elected by the clergy assigned to each cathedral (the chapter). At times factions would vie for a majority of votes in a manner which, to put it

119

mildly, was unedifying. As a corrective, the Third Lateran Council (1170) decreed that in all the world's dioceses, the electors more noted for their virtue, zeal, and disinterestedness—the *sanior pars*—must all vote with the majority if the election was to be valid. Unanimity of the *sanior pars* was taken as a sign of divine endorsement of the elected candidate.[3]

The example illustrates the early theoretical conflict between modern majority rule and the more primitive search for truth.[4] Canon law showed a dual allegiance. On the one hand, everyone who was affected by a decision had a right to a voice in its approval. This is the Justinian's maxim *Quod omnes tangit ab omnibus approbetur.*[5] Balancing this introduction of diverse interests was an emphasis on the unity in truth which should prevail where the Spirit is active. One device for fostering such unity without disenfranchising those with a mere factional spirit was to demand that there be not merely a majority in favor of a candidate, but a majority including all who constituted the *sanior pars*.

The same principle emerged elsewhere in canonical thought. When the well-being of the whole diocesan corporation is in question, said the famous canonist Zabarella (*c.* 1335-1417), the bishop cannot act alone; he must have either the consent of the whole chapter or at least of its *major et sanior pars*.[6] This notion that God's will can be found in the unanimity of the most upright members of a decision making body has been traced through hundreds of years in the governance of the dioceses of Great Britain.[7]

But the flowering of medieval belief that the Spirit speaks in the unanimous actions of a governing body is the theory of Church Councils. As medieval political historian Brian Tierney has clearly demonstrated,[8] the principles of Conciliar theory in the fourteenth century derive directly from twelfth and thirteenth century canon law. Nicholas of Cusa, a fifteenth century political theorist and theologian, reflects the tension within that legal tradition between majoritarian and unitarian approaches. On occasion, Cusa alleges that the majority side always expresses the will of the Spirit.[9] He, however, cannot long remain satisfied with mere majority rule. In an attempted compromise of systems, Cusa "insists that the minority formally endorse the decision of the majority after the vote so as to produce the required unanimity especially in the definition of doctrine."[10]

But then Cusa confronted a practical problem. He was a member of the anti-papal Council of Basle (1431-1438). The majority voted to hold a council of reunion with the Greeks at Avignon; but there was deep disagreement by a minority of prelates (fifteen out of fifty-two present) whose honest zeal for reunion made them, in Cusa's eyes, the *senior* though far *minor pars*.[11] Cusa felt constrained to desert Basle and endorse the papal side. The Council of Basle, in spite of its large majorities, could not achieve the unity which is the mark of a true council. After all, Cusa had written long before Basle that "on account of the unanimity on which the authority of the acts of a council depends, we know that the Holy Spirit, who is the spirit of union and harmony [concordantiae] has inspired the council's decision.[12] Conversely, "where there is dissent, there is no council."[13]

The conciliar thought which Cusa enunciated so clearly, with its central emphasis on how the will of God was to be found in the unity behind the decrees of church councils, had direct impact on English parliamentary theory in the days of Henry VIII's establishment of a national church. Parliament emerged as an interim substitute for a worldwide church council and took on all the latter's attributes. One of Henry's most prominent apologists, Christopher St. German, wrote, "It cannot be thought that a Statute that is made by authority of the whole Realm, as well as of the King and of the Lords Spiritual and Temporal, as of all the commons, will recite a thing against the Truth."[14] Ecclesiastical historian George Hunston Williams sums up the argument: "The nation ultimately, Parliament representatively, was in the Henrician theory the King's body political *and ecclesiastic* as distinguished from his body natural. St. German regarded Parliament so conceived as a national mixed synod, guided by the Holy Spirit, and as such incapable of error, in effect, infallible. The King of Parliament, as it were, can do no wrong."[15]

Because of this approach, Anglicanism tended to consider Parliament as not only national diet but national synod.[16] One channel, therefore, by which Catholic conciliar infallibility reached Fox's England would be the conciliar rhetoric surrounding Parliament.[17]

The Anabaptist Tradition

An altogether independent channel of transmission to Fox's England was the nonmagisterial Protestant tradition, especially that of the Anabaptists. Divine inspiration was introduced dramatically by Henry Pfeiffer and Thomas Muntzer at Muhlhausen in 1525 when the two revolutionaries replaced the town council with the so-called eternal council representative of the revolutionary classes. Apparently, the people would elect pastors who in turn would deliberate in a council. The council would express the truths the people held but could not articulate.

This was to be an <u>eschatological</u> council, a *Konzil der Endzeit* which would establish true church order as the final step prior to the Second Coming of Christ. Although we do not know its decision making procedures, it certainly was supposed to produce decisions guaranteed by the Holy Spirit. Details are unclear since the eternal council was overthrown and Muntzer and Pfeiffer beheaded by Landgrave Philip of Hesse after only a few months.

In variant forms, the notion of an eschatological council continued to appear in the Radical Reformation. In August 1527, two other Anabaptist leaders, John Hut and John Denck, summoned a council (later termed the Martyrs' Synod) at Augsburg to discuss immediate preparations for the Second Coming which they hoped would occur on Pentecost Sunday the year following. Williams summed up their expectations: "As once in the upper room in Jerusalem the first apostolic council had convened and the flames of the Spirit had descended upon the participants, so in the fullness of the dispensations, the Spirit would come again in power, anointing the new apostles for the last days before the millenium."[18]

Yet another Anabaptist version of conciliar thought, exemplified by Balthasar Hubmaier who taught at Nicolsburg in Moravia in 1527, was that individual local churches may indeed err, but the universal church could not. Therefore he was ready to submit to truly universal council where the Spirit of God, which moved freely in each redeemed person, could offset by its dynamic presence the partiality of fleshly wills.

Finally, we might note the principle of the *Sitzerrecht* or *Lex Sedentium*—the belief much discussed among Anabaptists that the local community of the faithful Christians will be inspired by the Holy Spirit when together its members sought a common understanding of passages from Scripture.[19] Interest in this approach to inspired interpretation of Scripture remained alive in Anabaptist circles over the years.

We have concentrated on Anabaptist traditions precisely because this is probably the safest way to avoid being caught in a morass. The immediate origin of Quaker beliefs and practices has been argued with much vigor and little satisfaction for generations. It is difficult to determine these origins just because there are so many plausible candidates! Among the sects abounding in Britain just prior to Fox's time, a large number reveal one or the other of the doctrines that would appear in Quakerism. In general, what these sects have in common is that they appealed to the 50 percent of the populace who could be labelled masterless men and that they share at least some Anabaptist roots, enough at least so that the notion of divine inspiration of the united community would be part of their religious world. In discussing each group, we will emphasize the doctrines strongly affirmed by them which were to become mainstays of Quaker belief.

Possible Anabaptist Channels to Quaker Origins

Early Mystics

Quaker historians have traced the list of the sixteenth century Anabaptist mystics who already proclaimed the characteristic Quaker belief in direct inner communion of man with God and used such "Quaker" terms as the Inward Light, Inward Word, and Divine Seed.[20] But they can allege no direct link between these writers and George Fox. For example, William Braithwaite writes: "George Fox was not a reader of books other than the Bible, nor a student of movements, and he reveals in his writings very slight direct acquaintance with the formative literature of mystical religion. This is true also of Dewsbury, Nayler, Howgill, Burrough, and other early makers of Quakerism."[21]

Although Rufus M. Jones has difficulty finding much evidence of direct influence in the writings of these earliest Friends, it remains true that Judge Hotham, George Fox's protector, wrote a life of Boehme. Hotham's brother Charles, also an acquaintance of Fox, was Boehme's translator.

The Familists

A second candidate for an Anabaptist channel to the Quakers is Henry Nicholas's Family of Love or Familists. This group came to England late in the first half of the sixteenth century and sprang momentarily into prominence again during the Commonwealth. The community believed in an Inner Light and held strongly that, contrary to Calvin and Luther, inner perfection could be attained by every man. In addition to these central "Quaker" tenets, the Familists foreshadowed Quakers in such particulars as their refusal to take oaths, opposition to war and capital punishment, dislike of ceremonious worship, preference for simple speaking, and marriage without an officiating minister. Yet the Familists did practice water baptism and had a hierarchy of rulers. Their exact mode of worship remains in doubt.[22]

Although many early Quaker recruits did in fact come from Familist backgrounds and some unusual Familist doctrines (for example, the celestial flesh of Christ) appear in the second generation of Quaker writing, most of the beliefs Familists shared with Quakers were also shared with General Baptists or with Seekers. There is no evidence that George Fox had contact with Familists in the days of his own spiritual searching but plenty of indication that his early spiritual homes were among Baptists and Seekers. Church historian George Williams is certainly right when he comments that "morphologically . . . the English Familists represent a transitional stage between evangelical Anabaptism and the completely nonsacramental Spiritualism of Quakerism." He may be overstating his case, however, when he adds that "to a certain extent genetically" the Familists led into Quakerism. William Braithwaite's observation that any clear channel of Familist influence on Fox is "not yet discovered" remains as true today as when Braithwaite wrote in 1912.[23]

The Seekers

A third approach to Quaker genesis is that mysterious collection of silent worshippers known as Seekers. Holding that no true Church existed in their age of apostasy, they gathered to worship in silence and awaited new revelation. They refused even the Anabaptist sacraments of baptism and the Eucharist until such time as worthy ministers—men of apostolic calibre—should appear. There is indication that some Seekers eventually doubted that the sacraments would be needed even should the apostolic age be restored. Like other independent sects, the Seekers opposed labelling the days of the week and months of the year by their common names since these commemorated pagan deities. This, too, would eventually be a Quaker testimony.

Further evidence of Seeker influence upon Quakers is that the early name Friends took on themselves was Children of the Light, a name in vogue among Seekers. Since George Fox spent much time among Seekers in the period just before the foundation of Quakerism and gathered so many converts from Seekers, it is not hard to see why Rufus Jones concludes that Quaker worship procedures "apparently came from the societies of Seekers—in the northern counties of England." Arnold Lloyd goes further and suggests that the probable source of the Quaker decision making process was also a Seeker practice, although he provides no substantiation.[24]

(General) Baptists, Especially John Smyth

It is important to notice, however, that the situation may not be as straightforward as it appears to be. The peculiar title, Children of the Light, was not just a Seeker phrase; it also was in use among Continental

Anabaptists. Thomas Edwards, in his 1646 handbook of heresies, *Gangraena*, informed his readers that in the years just after 1640, the "Seekers greatly increased, Independent Baptists leaving their congregations; not only the people, but the ministers." Writing in the same year, Baillie affirmed that Spilsby, a Baptist leader, "acknowledges, that many Baptists become Seekers."[25] Although it would appear that the misty origins of Seekerism were native English, not Continental Baptist, by Fox's day the line between Baptist and Seeker may have been very easy to cross. Both Seekers and Baptists held the same doctrines, with the difference that Baptists practiced baptism and the Lord's Supper, Seekers did without them at least until worthy apostles might be raised up by God.

Such similarities between the two sects explains why Fox found the soil so fertile in both communities. His *Journal* records him preaching in 1647 and 1648 at various Baptist meetings. In 1649, he had a "loving" religious discussion with the celebrated Baptist preacher Samuel Oates and others. Steeplehouse—Fox's standard epithet for a church building—was not his own invention but the common usage among Baptists prior to Fox. Appropriately, William Braithwaite sees in the "broken" Baptist community at Nottinghamshire which Fox encountered in 1647-48 "the channel along which many of the Baptist influences which affected Quakerism probably came."[26] Rufus Jones urges that this same encounter "first supplied George Fox with congenial religious fellowship and, under his leadership, developed into the earliest Quaker congregation.[27] In support of this view one can cite such early sources as Ephraim Pagitt, Fox's contemporary, who wrote "the Quaker is an upstart branch of the Anabaptists."[28]

It would be good to underscore here that the (Ana)Baptists to which we have been referring are the group known in England as General Baptists. They held the Arminian notion that salvation was open to all men; opposing this view were the Particular Baptists who maintained a true Calvinist notion of predestination: only a few among earth's denizens were numbered among God's elect. Nottinghamshire, where Fox made his first convert and formed his first community, was the location of one of the two original communities of English General Baptists, and the neighborhood was heavily blessed with Baptist communities which owed their origins to the Baptist church founded by John Smyth two generations previously or to churches in communion with Smyth's group.[29]

John Smyth's Baptists are especially interesting. They began in England, but persecution forced Smyth to lead part of the community from Gainsborough to Amsterdam in 1607. His community, feeling very close in belief to Amsterdam's Waterlander Mennonite Church, united with the Mennonites in 1615, although maintaining separate services until 1639. This allegiance with the Mennonites reinforced Smyth's own theological growth. A strongly spiritualist dimension of the Waterlanders included disenchantment with prepared preaching, baptism, and communion in favor of silent meditation together. Smyth's writings reveal the language one would later find in Fox, that action was to be taken "for the cleering of the truth" and "that the truth wee walk in may be manifested." Worship was apparently to include much silence, spontaneous speaking by any member when moved by the Spirit, the exclusion of preestablished forms of worship such as reciting memorized prayers or even reading Scripture as part of the service. Thus:

> The Spirit is quenched by silence when fit matter is revealed to one that sitteth by and he withholdeth it in tyme of prophecying; the Spirit is quenched by sett formes of worship, for therein the spirit is not at liberty to utter it self, but is bounded in . . .; Saying set formes, of worship by rote is quenching the Spirit; & Reading sett formes or worship out of a book is quenching the Spirit; for in the one the Spirit is not manifested but the strength of the memory, in the other the matter is not brought out of the hart, but out of the book; & so in neyther of them the Spirit is at liberty.

The resemblance to a Quaker meeting for worship is manifest.

Even the mode of dealing with those who erred in their participation in the worship was similar. In 1608 Smyth said, "If any thing doubtful or false be delivered in type of spirituall worship it is to be examyned & censured afterward."[30] Fox would write in 1659 "that no Friends judge one another in meetings; but if any be moved to speak [to such,] to do it after meeting in private."[31]

Smyth, the father of English General Baptists, and his flock opposed going to law against other members, opposed the taking of oaths, found the morality of war dubious at best, urged the priority of the inward inspiration of God over the outward scripture, and allowed that if any believed in Christ's "celestial flesh," Smyth would *not* "refuse brotherhood with him."[32] This position by Smyth weakens considerably George Williams's argument that the source of the spiritual flesh theology of Robert Barclay and George Keith had to be the English Familists.[33] In all these positions, Smyth foreshadowed characteristic Quaker notions.

Even the idea that women should be allowed to preach—a basic tenet of Fox[34]—seems to have started in the Baptist churches of Holland. It reached American Baptists by 1636 and English Baptists by 1641.[35]

As far as governance was concerned, Anabaptists generally believed in discipline imposed by the community, for the community was a school where Christ was the Master. In theory, at least, the Anabaptist pastors and other leaders were not so powerful as officials of the magisterial reformation churches. Smyth added a dimension, again important for Quakerism, that the hierarchical arrangement of officers found among Presbyterians and other Amsterdam Baptists was dropped. Instead, there were simply two kinds of officers: pastors—who could perform such functions as teaching or governing—and deacons who worried about the practical details of the church.

This elimination of hierarchy among spiritual leaders had the practical effect of giving the congregation (which elected them) true authority over its elders in a way that had not been possible under a hierarchical structure.[36]

English Baptist communities added a variant to Smyth's two-level structure. Ministers were not entrusted with the guidance of a single community but travelled constantly. In practice, this seems to have diminished the authority of ministers in local matters and enhanced the local deacons.

The earliest Quaker communities of which we have clear record— those formed from Westmoreland Seekers in 1652 and 1653—seem to have adopted the Baptist pattern. Friends whose talent for preaching was singular were recognized and encouraged to travel among the communities as unordained ministers; each local community was governed by its own elders (overseers).[37]

Finally, Barclay cites a tantalizing letter describing the business meeting as conducted in Smyth's congregation. We learn that, although all those present "had free liberty of voting decisively, and of debate," yet "nothing must go by *number or plurality of voices,* and there must be no moderator, or prolocutor, for the order of their action."[38] It would appear that a meeting which proceeds without totalling the number of votes or seeking pluralities is, in essence, following the Quaker procedure sketched in the quotation at the head of this chapter. We *may* have in Smyth's practice the genesis of Quaker decision making.

It would be a great relief, of course, if we would now provide some document enlarging on Smyth's decision making procedure, showing that it continued to be in vogue among the General Baptists Fox met in 1647-48 or the Seekers in 1652, and that Fox, recognizing its appropriateness,

127

adopted it. No such magic document has been discovered. We are left with the possibility that Smyth's procedure did influence Fox. To be sure, the channel of influence could have been either the obvious one—through the Baptist communities Fox met—or the less expected route—through the Seeker communities with their large membership of former Baptists.

Uncertain as we are about the method of transmission, we can be more confident in claiming that, at a minimum, Smyth's congregation was the principal medium through which Continental Anabaptism was transferred into England. Part and parcel of that Anabaptism was the belief in divine guidance of communities seeking God's will together. George Fox and his early followers read little other than their Bibles. Their doctrine came from beliefs that were in the air and in the various religious communities which they visited. As Agnes Tierney wrote, "Indeed, there was hardly a truth in the message of Fox that hadn't been held by some sect either in England or on the Continent."[39] But Fox "discovered" the truths he was to preach through the gradual religious insights reported in his *Journal*. If today's scholar can suggest possible sources for Fox's ideas, there is no way to go beyond that and certify the particular genesis of each of those ideas.

Rufus Jones is helpful on this point:

> It may be taken for granted, I think, that Fox was unaware of his immense debt to the contemporary movements and spiritual interpreters. The ideas and central truths which burst into his consciousness as "openings," "insights," and "incursions" were in the air. They were in books and were being preached in closets, if not from house tops, but they were not real to Fox, and did not move him to action until they surged up *in him* and were born of his flesh and blood. . . . He did not originate the ideas which his movement incarnated, but he personally discovered them, identified himself with them, poured his life through them. . . .[40]

A Divinely-Inspired Army: The Putney Debates

As a final illustration of the extent to which divine guarantees of decision making were expected in the England of 1647, let us look at the advice offered by Oliver Cromwell at points of disagreement during the Putney debates of his Council of the Army.

The participants in these debates included State Church Presbyterians, Independent Congregationalists who shared much Presbyterian theology but advocated toleration of all sects, and sectaries with Anabaptist and other separatist allegiances who also sought toleration.

Cromwell first proposed that a committee be formed of spokesmen for all viewpoints to compare ideas "that we may understand really, as before God, the bottom of our desires, and that we may seek God together, and see if God will give us an uniting spirit." He urged that they agree to this procedure, for "I doubt not but, if in sincerity we are willing to submit to that light that God shall cast in among us, God will unite us, and make us of one heart and one mind."

Later the same day in 1647, Cromwell returned to the point. The group should adjourn "to seek the guidance of God, and to recover that presence of God that seems to withdraw from us." The differing parties would gather again the next afternoon "to see what God will direct you to say to us, that whilst we are going one way, and you another, we be not both destroyed. This required [guidance from the] Spirit."

A few days later, Cromwell opened the final Putney session by suggesting "that everyone might speak their experiences as the issue of what God had given, in answer to their prayers." After many had spoken, he remarked:

> Truly we have heard speaking to us; and I cannot but think that in many of those things God hath spoke to us. I cannot but think that in most that have spoke there hath been something of God laid forth to us; and yet there have been several contradictions in what hath been spoken. But certainly God is not the author of contradictions.

He concluded his remarks with his own criteria for spiritual discernment.

> I think that this law and this [word] speaking [within us], which truly is in every man who hath the Spirit of God, we are to have a regard to. And this to me seems to be very clear, how we are to judge of the apprehension of men [as] to particular cases, whether it be of God or no. When it doth not carry its evidence with it, of the power of God to convince us clearly, our best way is to judge the conformity or disformity of [it with] the law written within us, which is the law of the Spirit of God, the mind of God, the mind of Christ. . . . I do not know any outward evidence of what proceeds from the Spirit of God more clear than this, the appearance of meekness and gentleness and mercy and patience and forbearance and love, and a desire to do good to all, and to destroy none that can be saved.[41]

Indeed, reliance on the Spirit for major decision making was in the air. Notice, however, that Cromwell's procedure, although it seeks unity, does not require it prior to taking action. Note, too, that Cromwell cannot simply state, as would George Fox, that there is something of God speaking in every man; for Cromwell, one should only listen to "every man who hath the Spirit"—which is a more appropriately Calvinist turn of phrase consistent with nonuniversal predestination.

The criteria Cromwell offered for testing whether an utterance was from God or not were highly vague: one judges the "conformity or disformity" of the utterance with "the law written within us." Then Cromwell quickly employed the gentle *style* of speech as further gauge of whether the speech was true—a weak test indeed, since one's style of speech can be mere affectation. As is noted in Part One of this book, this ambiguity also plagued Fox and his coworkers.

Appendix B

A Quaker Glossary

Attender: Someone who participates in Quaker worship but who has not yet sought and gained membership in the meeting.

Centered: Condition of an individual or group in touch with the divine presence.

Covered Meeting: Condition found in a worshiping group when an awareness and presence of God is felt in its midst.

Clearness: Confidence that an action is consistent with the divine will.

Convinced Friend: A person who has been converted to Quakerism.

Disorderly Walkers: Quakers whose conduct is contrary to the community's ethical standards.

Disownment: Excommunication; loss of membership in the monthly meeting.

First Day: Sunday.

First Publishers of Truth (Valiant Sixty): A group of sixty itinerant preachers who, with George Fox, were the initial preachers of the Quaker gospel. Twelve of these First Publishers were women.

Gathered Meeting: see *Covered Meeting.*

In the Life: An insight or decision reached under the influence of God.

Inner Light: The presence of Christ (that of God) in every person.

Leadings: The sense of divine guidance or revelation in any action.

Meeting House: The Quaker equivalent of a church building. The term is intended to be suggestive of simplicity.

Meeting for Business: A gathering of Friends for the purpose of making business decisions.

Meeting for Sufferings: A body selected to do the work of London Yearly Meeting when the latter is not in session.

Meeting for Worship: A gathering of Friends for the purpose of worship.

Minute: A summary statement of an agreement reached in a meeting for business.

Monthly Meeting: A local community of Friends (akin to a parish) in which membership resides. So named because, by custom, the community meets once a month to conduct a meeting for business.

Opening: see *Leading.*

Quarterly Meeting: A regional unit, comprised of two or more monthly meetings, which meets on a quarterly basis to conduct a meeting for business.

Representative Meeting: A body selected to do the work of a yearly meeting when the latter is not in session; the American equivalent of London Yearly Meeting's Meeting for Sufferings.

Sense of the Meeting: The harmony (union, unity) reached by participants in a business meeting.

Truth: A synonym for Christ or the divine guide; the complex of Quaker ethical traditions; the Quaker gospel.

Valiant Sixty: see *First Publishers of Truth.*

Yearly Meeting: An annual gathering for worship and business open to members of all monthly meetings within a large region. This body is akin to a diocese in other Christian communities, but with advisory rather than determinative authority over smaller units. A yearly meeting may have a staff which provides services to monthly and quarterly meetings, represents the yearly meeting to the general public, and carries on the projects initiated by the annual meeting.

Yearly Meeting Friends: Quakers known for involvement at the yearly meeting level.

Notes

Part I Chapter I

1. Rufus M. Jones, *Mysticism and Democracy* (Cambridge, Massachusetts: Harvard University Press, 1932), p. 56.

2. George Fox, *The Journal of George Fox,* ed. John L. Nickalls (Cambridge: Cambridge University Press, 1952), p. 56.

3. William C. Braithwaite, *The Beginnings of Quakerism* (London: Macmillan, 1912), p. 426. Christopher Hill, *The World Turned Upside Down* (New York: Viking, 1973), pp. 33-34, 163.

4. Fox, *Journal,* p. 263.

5. Abram R. Barclay, *Letters of Early Friends* (London: Harvey and Darton, 1841), pp. 310, 297. Burrough says he came to London nine years previous (1653) and that the Meeting was established two years later [Cf. William C. Braithwaite, *Spiritual Guidance in Quaker Experience* (London: Swarthmore Press, 1909) p. 64]. Braithwaite claims the summer of 1656 for the establishment of the meeting in his *The Beginnings of Quakerism* p. 320. Arnold Lloyd suggests 1652, but with no documentation in his *Quaker Social History,* (New York: Longmans, 1950).

6. Abram R. Barclay, *Letters,* p. 298.

7. Ibid., p. 305.

8. Ibid.

9. *Quaker Strongholds* (n.p., 1891), pp. 11-13, cited in London Yearly Meeting, *Christian Faith and Practice in the Experience of the Society of Friends* (Richmond, Indiana: Friends United Press, 1973), par. 80.

10. Robert Barclay, *Barclay's Apology in Modern English,* ed. Dean Freiday (Philadelphia: Friends Book Store, 1967), proposition 2, sec. 7, pp. 357, 355-356. In order to clarify Barclay's argument, we use Freiday's excellent edition whenever possible. Propositions and sections are indicated for the benefit of a reader using some other edition.

11. Fox, *Journal,* p. 145; see also pp. 179, 218, 224, 225.

12. Rufus M. Jones, *New Studies in Mystical Religion* (New York: Macmillan, 1927), p. 170. Rufus M. Jones, *Quakerism, A Spiritual Movement* (Philadelphia: Philadelphia Yearly Meeting, 1963), p. 87.

13. Howard H. Brinton, *Friends for 300 Years* (New York: Harper and Brothers, 1952), pp. xiii, p. 63.

14. *Quaker Fundamentals,* p. 6, quoted in Henry Van Etten, *George Fox and the Quakers* (New York: Harper Torchbooks, 1959), p. 164.

15. Robert Barclay, *Apology,* proposition 2, sec. 7, p. 356. Italics in original.

16. Richard T. Vann, *The Social Development of English Quakerism 1655-1755* (Cambridge, Massachusetts: Harvard University Press, 1969) pp. 112-113. The words in the second set of quotation marks are taken from the minutes themselves.

17. London Yearly Meeting, *Christian Life, Faith and Thought in the Society of Friends* (London: Friends Book Centre, 1943). The quoted material from Besse's *Sufferings* (n.p. 1753), vol. 2, pp. 201-202, was written in jail eight days prior to the execution.

18. Fox, *Journal,* p. 27. Cf. Fox's similar responses to a court in 1652 on p. 135.

19. Ibid., p. 27.

20. Hill, *The World Turned,* pp. 190-191, 47, 60, 163, 22.

21. London Yearly Meeting, *Christian Life,* p. 15.

22. Hill, *World Turned,* p. 200.

23. B. Nicholson, *A Blast from the Lord* (1653) quoted by J. F. Maclear, "Quakerism and the End of the Interregnum," *Church History* 19:245.

24. Francis Howgill, *A Woe to Magistrates* (1654) quoted by Hill, *World Turned,* p. 196.

25. James Nayler, *Wisdom from Beneath* (1653) quoted by Hill, *World Turned,* p. 196.

26. George Fox and James Nayler, *Several Papers* (1654), p. 23; quoted by Hill, *World Turned,* p. 199.

27. Abram R. Barclay, *Letters of Early Friends* (London: Harvey and Darton, 1841), p. 311. Fox is writing in 1689. The term, "monthly meeting," which refers to the special session for business held each month by local Quaker communities, *may* be loose usage here as the tradition of meeting monthly for business sessions may not have emerged in many districts before Fox's 1654 campaign. Van Etten, for example, flatly asserts, "There was no such thing as a form of organization among the children of the Light, Fox's first followers." (Van Etten, *George Fox,* pp. 77-78.) Robert Barclay, the historian, seems to claim that there were no such sessions prior to 1652 at Sedberg. (Robert Barclay, *The Inner Life of the Religious Societies of the Commonwealth,* 3rd ed. (London: Hodden and Stoughton, 1879), p. 351.

28. Fox, *Journal,* pp. 107-109, 22-23.

29. Swarthmore MSS, 3, 19, cited in Arnold Lloyd, *Quaker Social History,* (New York: Longmans, 1950), p. 2. Boswell Middleton MS., p. 26; cited in Lloyd, *Quaker Social History,* p. 1.

30. Portfolio 36, p. 19, cited in Lloyd, *Quaker Social History,* p. 2.

31. Vann, *The Social Development,* p. 138. Abram R. Barclay, *Letters,* p. 298. Cf. Van Etten, *George Fox,* p. 77.

32. Fox, *Journal,* p. 215.

33. Harold Loukes urges that such "settling" probably meant establishing monthly meetings. *The Discovery of Quakerism* (London: Harrop, 1960) p. 63. Cf. Fox, *Journal*, p. 174.

34. William Wistar Comfort, *William Penn's Religious Background* (Ambler, Pennsylvania: Upper Dublin United Monthly Meeting, 1944), p. 12.

35. G. M. Trevelyan, *English Social History*, p. 267, cited by Taylor, *Valiant Sixty*, pp. 74-75.

36. Fox, *Journal*, p. 280.

37. Ibid., pp. 280-281.

38. Ibid., pp. 281-285.

39. William C. Braithwaite, *The Beginnings*, pp. 338-339.

40. Abram R. Barclay, *Letters*, p. 284. Cf. Lloyd, *Quaker Social History*, p. 21.

41. Hill, *World Turned*, p. 279.

42. John Audland, *The Innocent Delivered Out of the Snare* (n.p. 1658), p. 33, cited in Hill, *World Turned*, p. 196.

43. J. A. Atkinson, ed., *Tracts Relating to the Civil War in Cheshire (1641-1659)* (n.p.: Chetham Society, 1909), p. 186, cited in Hill, *World Turned*, p. 280. Cf. p. 199 and Cf. Hugh Barbour, *The Quakers in Puritan England* (New Haven: Yale University Press, 1964), pp. 199-206.

44. A. L. Morton, *The World of the Ranters* (London: Lawrence and Wishart, 1970), pp.. 18-19.

45. Hill, *World Turned*, pp. 203, 283.

46. Twenty-one Quakers died from persecution before April 1659; over three hundred died during the Restoration period. See Braithwaite, *Beginnings*, p. 465.

47. Fox, *Journal*, p. 398. Braithwaite suggests the number 4,230 in *The Second Period of Quakerism* (London: Macmillan, 1919), p. 9.

48. Fox, *Journal*, p. 399.

49. Hill, *World Turned*, p. 194.

50. Braithwaite, *Second Period*, p. 13.

51. Max Weber, *From Max Weber: Essays in Sociology*, eds. H. H. Gerth and C. Wright Mills (New York: Oxford University Press, 1958).

52. Fox, *Journal*, pp. 285n, 372, See Braithwaite, *Beginnings*, p. 338.

53. *Reliquiae Baxterianae*, vol. 1, pp. 436-437, cited in Hill, *World Turned*, p. 168. Cf. Brinton, *Friends*, p. 158.

54. Loukes treats the controversy as "quaint" in *Discovery*, p. 63; Van Etten calls it "quite unimportant" in *George Fox*, p. 76; even Fox's principal contemporary defender admits to his own initial prejudice against Fox. Kenneth E. Carroll, *John Perrot: Early Quaker Schismatic* (London: Friends Historical Society, 1971), p. vii. Braithwaite, *Beginnings*, p. 275.

55. Braithwaite, *Second Period*, p. 233.

56. Fox, *Journal*, p. 268.

57. *Epistles and Advices of George Fox to Birmingham Friends* (n.p. 1681), cited in Lloyd, *Quaker Social History,* pp. 178-179. See Braithwaite, *Second Period,* p. 242.

58. John Bolton, *Judas and His Treachery* (London: n.p., 1670), pp. 18-19, cited in Carroll, *Perrot,* p. 61.

59. John Perrot, *To All Simple, Honest-Intending and Innocent People* (London: n.p., 1664), p. 6, cited in Carroll, *Perrot,* p. 78.

60. Carroll, *Perrot,* pp. 57-58, 55, 75, 60, 50. See Braithwaite, *Second Period,* p. 237.

61. Braithwaite, *Second Period,* p. 244.

62. Carroll, *Perrot,* pp. 64, 65. See Braithwaite, *Second Period,* p. 235.

63. George Fox, *The Spirit of Envy, Lying, and Persecution Made Manifest* (London: n.p., 1664), p. 13, quoted in Carroll, *Perrot,* p. 65.

64. Carroll, *Perrot,* p. 77. See Braithwaite, *Second Period,* p. 240.

Part I Chapter II

1. Abram R. Barclay, *Letters,* p. 321. Carroll. *Perrot,* pp. 82, 91. See Lloyd, *Quaker Social History,* p. 24.

2. Braithwaite, *Second Period,* p. 248.

3. Brinton, *Friends,* p. 101.

4. Kenneth Carroll lists twenty-one of the leading supporters of Perrot in a catalog he describes as a "Quaker Who's Who." See Carroll, *Perrot,* pp. 87-89, 91.

5. Fox, *Journal,* pp. 510-511, 505-507, 510. It would appear that, in some areas, custom had changed during the persecution to holding meeting for business only quarterly. See Brathwaite, *Second Period,* p. 251.

6. Braithwaite, *Second Period,* p. 276.

7. Fox, *Journal,* p. 511. See Carroll, *Perrot,* pp. 92-94.

8. Brinton, *Friends,* p. 101. See Vann, *Social Development,* p. 91.

9. Fox, *Journal,* p. xlvii. Edited by John L. Nickalls (London Yearling Meeting).

10. Swarthmore Collection, vol. 5, p. 9, quoted in Braithmore, *Second Period,* p. 280.

11. Fox, *Journal,* p. 20-21, 14.

12. Karl Rahner and Herbert Vorgrimler, *Theological Dictionary* (New York: Seabury Press, 1965), p. 72.

13. Fox, *Journal,* p. 35.

14. Braithwaite, *Beginnings,* p. 26.

15. William Allen, *The Danger of Enthusiasm Discovered in an Epistle to the Quakers* (London: Barbazon Aylmer, 1674), p. 12.

16. Ibid, p. 96.

17. Van Etten, *George Fox,* p. 14.

18. George Fox and Thomas Lawrence, *Concerning Marriage* (n.p., 1663), p. 10,

cited in J. William Frost, *The Quaker Family in Colonial America* (New York: St. Martin's Press, 1973), p. 20.

19. Braithwaite, *Spiritual Guidance*, p. 51.

20. Hill, *World Turned*, p. 225. He went through the streets crying, "Woe unto the bloody Lichfield." See Fox, *Journal*, p. 71.

21. Braithwaite, *Spiritual Guidance*, pp. 40-41, 55.

22. For discussions of the dilemma, consult Braithwaite, *Second Period*, p. 250 and Braithwaite, *Beginnings*, p. 109.

23. Braithwaite, *Beginnings*, p. 147.

24. Abram R. Barclay, *Letters*, pp. 358, 355-356.

25. Barbour, *Quakers in Puritan England*, p. 119.

26. Braithwaite, *Spiritual Guidance*, p. 57.

27. Braithwaite, *Beginnings*, p. 150. See Roland H. Bainton, *The Travail of Religious Liberty* (Philadelphia: Westminster Press, 1951), p. 128.

28. Vernon Noble, *The Man in Leather Breeches* (New York: Philosophical Library, 1953), p. 79.

29. Braithwaite, *Second Period*, p. 339. Christopher Hill, a non-Quaker student of the period, reassures us that, when Quakers "went naked for a sign," they wore "only a loincloth about their middles for decency." Unfortunately, Hill does not document his assertion. See Hill, *World Turned*, p. 256.

30. Bainton, *Travail*, p. 128.

31. For examples, the reader might well skim I Corinthians and II Corinthians.

32. Frost, *Quaker Family*, p. 24; see Genesis. 6:1-4, 24:4, 26:35.

33. Ibid, p. 34, 40, 33.

34. *Gospel-Truth*, pp. 131, 138, quoted in Hill, *World Turned*, pp. 212-213.

35. Robert Barclay, *Apology*, proposition 3, sec. 7, p. 62. Italics in original.

36. Carroll, *Perrot*, p. 85. See Frost. *Quaker Family*, p. 25.

37. ARBARC./73, Warmsworth, Oct. 13, 1659, cited in Barbour, *Quakers in Puritan England*, p. 120.

38. Robert Barclay, *The Anarchy of the Ranters* (Philadelphia: Joseph Crukshank, 1770), p. 72. Brinton, *Friends*, p. 49. *Galatians*, 5:22. Abram R. Barclay, *Letters*, pp. 336, 341, 403-404. Henry Cadbury, *George Fox's Book of Miracles* (Cambridge: Cambridge University Press, 1912), pp. 112-114.

39. Robert Barclay, *Apology*, proposition 2, sec. 12, p. 370, sec. 10, p. 366. Italics.

40. Fox, *Journal*, p. xliii.

41. Frost, *Quaker Family*, p. 13. For Braithwaite's confirming judgment, see *Spiritual Guidance*, p. 52.

42. Jacques Guillet et al., *Discernment of Spirits* (Collegeville, Minnesota: Liturgical Press, 1970).

43. Ignatius Loyola, *The Spiritual Exercises*, trans. Louis J. Puhl, S. J.

(Westminster, Maryland: Newman Press, 1951), nos. 176, 313-336, 170.

44. John Carroll Futrell, *Making an Apostolic Community of Love* (St. Louis, Missouri: Institute of Jesuit Sources, 1970), pp. 193-194.

45. Braithwaite, *Spiritual Guidance*, p. 66; See Van Etten, *George Fox*, p. 77.

46. *The Spirit of the Hat* (n.p., 1673), cited in Braithwaite, *Second Period*, pp. 292, 293.

47. Braithwaite, *Second Period*, pp. 294, 297-298.

48. "Meetings for Discipline" in MS "Books of Extracts," quoted in Ibid., p. 348.

49. *Yearly Meeting Printed Epistles*, vol. 1 (1681-1769), pp. li-lvi, printed in Ibid., p. 309.

50. MS "Christian and Brotherly Advices," p. 105, cited in Lloyd, *Quaker Social History*, p. 28.

51. MS. "Minutes of the Yearly Meeting," vol. 1, p. 66, quoted in Lloyd, *Quaker Social History*, p. 28.

52. Works, p. 238, cited in Braithwaite, *Second Period*, p. 340.

53. Lloyd, *Quaker Social History*, pp. 26, 27.

54. Robert Barclay, *Anarchy*, pp. 84-89, 98, 102, 105, 109.

55. Allen, *Danger*, p. 91.

56. Robert Barclay, *Anarchy*, p. 91, 24-25.

57. Ibid, pp. 58-64, 21, 65-68, 74.

58. Thomas Crisp, *The First Part of Babel's Builders Unmasking Themselves* (1682), cited in Braithwaite, *Second Period*, p. 349.

59. Yearly Meeting Minutes, 17.iii.1695 and George Keith, *The Plea of the Innocent* (n.p., 1692); both cited in Lloyd, *Quaker Social History*, p. 137.

60. Braithwaite, *Second Period*, pp. xxxi, 386.

61. Ibid, p. xli. Jones divides the blame somewhat: Continental Quietism later reinforces the damage Barclay does. See Jones, *Spiritual Movement*, p. 156.

62. Braithwaite, *Second Period*, p. xxxvi, xlv, xxxv.

63. Braithwaite, *Second Period*, p. xliv. See Jones, *Spiritual Movement*, pp. 158-159.

64. Lloyd, *Quaker Social History*, p. 123.

65. Robert Barclay, *Apology*, proposition 4, sec. 4, p. 94; proposition 6, sec. 24, p. 176 and proposition 5, sec. 21, p. 162; proposition 11, pp. 348-409 passim.

66. Abram R. Barclay, *Letters*, p. 219.

67. Fox and Lawrence, *Concerning Marriage*, p. 12, cited in Frost, *Quaker Family* p. 14.

68. Braithwaite, *Second Period*, p. 383.

69. Fox, *Journal*, p. 27. See Braithwaite, *Spiritual Guidance*, p. 35.

70. Dean Freiday, "Not a Steeple, a Steeple, a Steeple," *Friends' Quarterly*, 18 (October 1974): 380-381.

71. Lloyd, *Quaker Social History,* p. 123.

72. Minutes of Yearly Meeting, vol. 1, 4th, 4th mo., 1675, cited in N.C. Hunt, *Two Early Political Associations* (Oxford: Clarendon Press, 1961), p. 3.

73. Minutes of Meeting for Sufferings, vol. 1, 18th, 8th mo., 1675, cited in Ibid., p. 3.

74. Ibid., p. 26, Cf. pp. 4, 7-10, 12, 15.

75. Ibid., chaps. 3-6.

76. Matthew 5:34. Minutes of Meeting for Sufferings, vol. 10, 12th, 12th mo., 1695/6, cited in Ibid, p. 50.

77. Minutes of Meeting for Sufferings, vol. 21, 4th, 3rd mo., 1715, cited in Ibid., p. 52.

78. Ibid., p. 53.

79. Minutes of Meeting for Sufferings, vol. 26, 17th, 1st mo., 1735/6, cited in Ibid., p. 90.

80. Braithwaite, *Second Period,* p. 516.

81. Ibid.

82. Paul R. Lawrence and Jay W. Lorsch, *Organization and Environment* (Boston: Harvard University Press, 1967), p. 209. See p. 185.

83. Ibid., pp. 192-193.

84. Ibid., p. 194.

85. For the early history of Quakerism in the Philadelphia Yearly Meeting area, the reader might consult *Friends in the Delaware Valley,* ed. John M. Moore (Haverford, Pennsylvania: Friends Historical Association, 1981).

Part II Chapter I

1. London Yearly Meeting, *Christian Faith and Practice in the Experience of the Society of Friends* (Richmond, Indiana: Friends United Press, 1973), frontispiece. Philadelphia Yearly Meeting, *Faith and Practice* (Philadelphia: Philadelphia Yearly Meeting, 1972), frontispiece.

2. Philadelphia Yearly Meeting, *Faith and Practice,* 1972, pp. 17-18.

3. London Yearly Meeting, *Christian Faith and Practice,* 1960, par. 353.

4. James F. Walker, "The Quaker Meeting for Business," *Pendle Hill Bulletin* 190 (April 1967):1-3. Cf. London Yearly Meeting, *Church Government* (London: Friends Book Centre, 1968), par. 716.

5. Thomas S. Brown, *When Friends Attend to Business* (Philadelphia: Philadelphia Yearly Meeting, n.d.), unpaginated. Cf. Douglas V. Steere, "The Quaker Decisionmaking Process," paper presented to Guilford College faculty, 12 February, 1975.

6. Steere, "Quaker Decisionmaking Process," p. 3. Cf. London Yearly Meeting, *Church Government,* par. 715.

7. D. Elton Trueblood, "The Quaker Method of Reaching Decisions," in *Beyond Dilemmas*, ed. S. B. Laughlin (New York: Lippincott, 1937), pp. 122-123.

8. Burton R. Clark, *The Distinctive College: Antioch, Reed, and Swarthmore* (Chicago, Aldine, 1970), p. 214.

9. Stuart Chase, *Roads to Agreement* (New York: Harper, 1951) pp. 51-52.

Part II Chapter II

1. Trueblood, "Quaker Method," p. 123.

2. Chase, *Roads*, p. 49. See London Yearly Meeting, *Church Government*, par. 720.

3. Margaret H. Bacon, *The Quiet Rebels* (New York: Basic Books, 1969), p. 174.

4. Glenn Bartoo, "Quaker Decisions," (Masters Dissertation, University of Chicago, 1952), p. 101.

5. To protect confidentiality, all quotations from interviews will appear in quotation marks, but without attribution.

6. Clark, *Distinctive College*, p. 173.

7. Representative Meeting, 24th, 4th mo. 1975.

8. Francis Pollard, Beatrice Pollard, and Robert Pollard, *Democracy and the Quaker Method* (London: Bannisdale Press, 1949), p. 62.

9. Brown, *When Friends*, unpaginated.

10. Walker, "Quaker Meeting for Business," unpaginated.

11. London Yearly Meeting, *Christian Faith and Practice*, par. 353.

12. Howard Haines Brinton, *Reaching Decisions: The Quaker Method* (Wallingford, Pa.: Pendle Hill, n.d.), p. 17.

13. Representative Meeting, 27th, 2nd mo., 1975.

14. Howard H. Brinton, *Creative Worship* (Wallingford, Pa.: Pendle Hill, 1963), pp. 93-94. Cf. Pollard, *Democracy*, p. 52. For remnants of that earlier atmosphere, see Bacon, *Quiet Rebels*, pp. 203-205.

Part II Chapter III

1. Cf. Bartoo, "Quaker Decisions," pp. 113, 114.

2. AR Barc./73, Warmsworth, October 13, 1659, cited in Barbour, *Quakers in Puritan England*, p. 120. See J. Milton Yinger, *The Scientific Study of Religion* (New York: Macmillan, 1970), p. 104.

3. Abram R. Barclay, *Letters*, p. 305. Much earlier, Nicholas of Cusa had singled out that the Holy Spirit, "who is the spirit of union and concord" led church councils to agreement without dissent. *De Concordantia Catholica*, 2.15.170. Cf. Paul E. Sigmund, *Nicholas of Cusa and Medieval Political Thought* (Cambridge, Massachusetts: Harvard University Press, 1963), p. 227.

4. Oxford English Dictionary, 1971, ed., s.v., "concordance."

5. Steere, "Quaker Decisionmaking," p. 4.

6. Bartoo, "Quaker Decisions," p. 67.

7. G. Von Schulze Gaevernitz, *Democracy and Religion* (London: George Allen and Unwin, 1930), p. 24.

8. A phenomenon common in groups which operate by voting seems to apply here as well, but with somewhat less significance. The individual who withdraws his objection or merely remains silent on a proposal he is known to oppose can expect that those now on the dominant side will do the same in his favor some day when they are in the minority on an issue. They owe him a debt for his cooperation. Thus, the individual who is weighing his leverage over the group might accede to the majority on a series of minor issues in order to build up enough debts to force the group to go in his direction on some matter of great importance to him.

Our observations lead us to conclude that such conduct goes on informally in matters of little moment: I agree to your committee's proposal for a picnic and I expect you to endorse my committee's proposal that the monthly meeting join the local ministerial alliance.

Major issues are another matter. Here Friends report that such a procedure—clearly opposed to the principle of selflessly seeking the Truth in the alternatives offered the group—would be most inappropriate. The decisions this writer has observed over many sessions of the same meetings, e.g., Representative Meeting from October 1974 to May 1975, give no reason to believe that such behavior is at all common.

9. Philadelphia Yearly Meeting, Sessions Six and Seven, 28th, 3rd mo., 1975.

10. After his personal observations of Friends came to an end, the writer was informed that the incident's outcomes were more significant than had appeared at first. At the subsequent meeting to decide on allotment of the budget quota among the monthly meetings, the objectors from the dissatisfied meeting continued their fight. Eventually, the "slighted" meeting refused to pay its share of the Yearly Meeting budget. One ought not think that the clerk's speed caused this major conflict within the community. Rather, the clerk's action merely offered the occasion for transition from an ongoing but informal conflict of philosophy to a public dispute. The sense of "failure of due process" seems to have contributed to the unhappy meeting's feeling of justification in refusing to accept the decision of the subsequent meeting called to distribute shares of the financial burden according to each meeting's ability to pay.

11. The passage of time often mellows memories and invites wit. One of the participants commented years later that it is amazing how "the topic of cohabitation can make estranged bedfellows of a body of Quakers."

12. Cf. Howard H. Brinton, *Guide to Quaker Practice* (Wallingford, Pa.: Pendle Hill, 1946), pp. 37-38.

13. Brinton, *Creative Worship*, p. 91.

Part II Chapter IV

1. Interview.

2. Henry Nash Smith, *Virgin Land* (New York: Vintage, 1950), p. v.

3. Rahner and Vorgrimler, *Theological Dictionary*, p. 303.

4. Stanley Ellin, "An Open Letter to All Friends," *Friends Journal* (January 1, 1976), p. 10. Cf. Henry J. Cadbury, *The Character of a Quaker* (Wallingford, Pa.: Pendle Hill, 1959), p. 24.

5. Bartoo, "Quaker Decisions," p. 62.

6. Blanche W. Shaffer, ed., *No Time But This Present* (Birmingham: Friends World Committee for Consultation, 1965), pp. 88-89.

7. L. Hugh Doncaster, *The Quaker Message; A Personal Affirmation* (Wallingford, Pa.: Pendle Hill, 1972), p. 5.

8. See the case of the Jewish Quaker in Bacon, *Quiet Rebels*, p. 207.

9. Shaffer, *No Time*, p. 48.

10. Ellin, "An Open Letter," p. 10.

11. Kathleen M. Slack, *Constancy and Change in the Society of Friends* (London: Friends Home Service Committee, 1967), pp. 43-44.

12. Howard E. Collier, *The Quaker Meeting* (Wallingford, Pa.: Pendle Hill, 1944), pp. 43-44.

13. Shaffer, *No Time*, p. 83.

14. Bartoo, "Quaker Decisions," p. 63. Italics in original.

15. Many allude to the Pollards' book as "worth reading along this line." See Pollard, *Democracy*, pp. 148-149 and 152-154.

16. Slack, *Constancy and Change*, p. 45.

17. Whether this Friend is right in discerning a shift to "explicit faith" is unclear. Certainly the Christocentric approach is generally respected among today's Friends if one uses the prominence of Christocentric Quakers in Philadelphia Yearly Meeting committees as a yardstick. This researcher was struck, however, by the number of universalist Friends who revealed little appreciation of recent developments in biblical research and therefore were unaware of the "passe" character of the science versus the Bible dispute. To such Friends, all Christocentrics tend to be lumped as benighted fundamentalists.

18. Rufus M. Jones, *Later Periods of Quakerism*, 2 vols. (London: Macmillan, 1921), 1:445.

19. Trueblood, "Quaker Method," p. 115.

20. Brinton, *Guide*, p. 41.

21. Thomas F. O'Dea, *The Mormons* (Chicago: University of Chicago Press, 1957) p. 86.

22. Philadelphia Friends use "thee" for nominative as well as accusative case.

23. Trueblood, "Quaker Method," p. 107. Rufus M. Jones, *Mysticism and*

Democracy (Cambridge, Massachusetts: Harvard University Press, 1932), p. 32. James D. Wilson, "Quakerism and the Democratic Process," *Quaker Life,* May, 1973, p. 27.

24. The speaker distinguished lower-level groups where the majority of participants are often not Quakers from higher more flexible units like the Board of Directors, all of whose members are by statute Friends. This observer noted a similar flexibility among monthly meetings and Philadelphia Yearly Meeting committees; in most cases a turn to silent reflection or a "delay until everybody's comfortable" produced a tempering of individual priorities even among those Friends most heavily committed to their own special interest.

25. Brown, *When Friends,* unpaginated.

26. Trueblood, "Quaker Method," p. 113.

27. Atypical but interesting was the gentleman of mature years who sat next to this observer during a session of 1975 Yearly Meeting. At the clerk's call for silent reflection, my neighbor picked up the *Philadelphia Bulletin* and read the comic strips until the day's business began.

28. Princeton Monthly Meeting, Meeting for Business, 4th, 5th mo., 1975.

29. Pollard, *Democracy,* p. 127.

30. Lewis Carroll, *The Annotated Alice,* ed. Martin Gardner (New York: Clarkson N. Potter, 1960), p. 269.

31. For example, Ellin, "Open Letter." An attempt to reconcile the two groups is T. Canby Jones, ed., *Quaker Understanding of Christ and of Authority* (Philadelphia: Friends World Committee for Consultation, 1974).

32. Philadelphia Yearly Meeting, Session 1, 21st, 3rd mo., 1975.

33. For example, Elias Hicks, *Journal of the Life and Religious Labours of Elias Hicks* (New York: Isaac T. Hooper, 1832).

Part II Chapter V

1. Steere, "Quaker Decisionmaking," p. 4. The reader should note Steere's use of "he or she/" Women frequently serve as clerks and are often noted for the sensitivity with which they carry out the task.

2. The clerk of Yearly Meeting and clerk of Representative Meeting prepare agenda with their Planning Committee and Executive Committee respectively. In monthly meeting, the clerk consults the overseers, sometimes in only an informal manner. In less regular meetings, consultation is less likely.

3. London Yearly Meeting, *Church Government,* par. 726.

4. Bartoo, *"Quaker Decisions,"* p. 35.

5. Brinton, *Guide,* p. 37.

6. Brinton, *Guide,* p. 37.

7. London Yearly Meeting, *Church Government,* par. 726.

8. Princeton Monthly Meeting, Meeting for Business, 2nd, 2nd mo., 1975.

9. Douglas M. McGregor, "The Human Side of Enterprise" in *Organizational Behavior and Management*, eds, Donald E. Porter and Philip B. Applewhite. (Scranton: International Textbook Company, 1964), pp. 453 and 454.

10. Ibid., pp. 455, 459-460.

11. London Yearly Meeting, *Church Government*, par. 721. Cf. Robert K. Greenleaf, *Servant Leadership* (Ramsey, New Jersey: Paulist Press, 1977).

12. I Cor. 12-14 and Rahner and Vorgrimler, *Theological Dictionary*, p. 72.

13. Minutes of Representative Meeting for 22nd, 10th mo., 1970: Minute 11.

14. Minutes of Representative Meeting for 3rd, 12th mo., 1970 and Interview.

15. Friends who explicitly accept either a Christological or a universalist understanding of the special quality of the gathered meeting have no difficulty verbalizing their religious acceptance of a decision made under the circumstances we describe here. Others whose membership in Friends does not seem to include the experiential quality of Friends worship are sometimes hard-pressed to deal with the sort of event we are discussing. Said one, "I don't go in much for that stuff; but you sure have to admit something odd is happening."

Conclusion

1. "Report of Representative Meeting to Clerks of Monthly Meetings," 3rd, 2nd mo., 1977.

2. Proceedings of Philadelphia Yearly Meeting, 1981 (Philadelphia: Philadelphia Yearly Meeting, 1981).

3. Calvin Wall Redekop, *The Old Colony Mennonites: Dilemmas of Ethnic Minority Life* (Baltimore: Johns Hopkins Press, 1969).

4. Richard A. Falk, *Future Worlds* (New York: Foreign Policy Association, 1976), p. 7. For a sketch of how the national viewpoints would have to be changed, see pp. 47-54.

5. Warren G. Bennis and Philip E. Slater, *The Temporary Society* (New York: Harper and Row, 1968).

6. Roberto Mangabeira Unger, *Knowledge and Politics* (New York: Free Press, 1975), p. 19.

7. Ibid., pp. 15, 21-24.

8. Alfred North Whitehead, *Adventures of Ideas* (New York: Free Press, 1933), p. 171.

Appendix A

1. Acts 15:25, 28 (King James).

2. Robert Barclay, *Anarchy*, p. 21.

3. Joseph A. McCallin, "The Development of a Legal Theory of Majority Rule in Elections," *Saint Louis University Law Journal* 16 (Fall 1971): 1-10.

4. Paul E. Sigmund, *Nicholas of Cusa*, p. 146.

5. Gaines Post, *Studies in Medieval Legal Thought* (Princeton, New Jersey: Princeton University Press, 1964), chap. 4.

6. *Lectura ad III. 7. 15* fol. 414b; cited in Brian Tierney, *Foundations of the Conciliar Theory* (Cambridge, Massachusetts: Cambridge University Press, 1955), p. 116.

7. For practical English applications of this principle, see Kathleen Edwards, *The English Secular Cathedrals in the Middle Ages* (Manchester: n.p., 1949), pp. 97-135, cited in Tierney, *Conciliar Theory*, p. 112.

8. Tierney, *Conciliar Theory*, pp. 220-237.

9. *De Concordantia Catholica*, 1.8.63: "Quare corpus sacerdotale, licet caducum et mortale at deviabile in memberis, non tamen in toto, quando semper major pars in fide et lege Christi permaneat . . .," cited in Sigmund, *Nicholas*, p. 146.

10. *De Concordantia Catholica*, 2.15.170, cited in Sigmund, *Nicholas*, p. 147.

11. Sigmund, *Nicholas*, pp. 224, 228.

12. *De Concordantia Catholica*, 2.10.138, cited in Ibid., p. 227.

13. "Qui enim sibi dissentiunt, non agunt concilium." *De Concordantia Catholica*, 2.1.93, cited in Sigmund, *Nicholas*, p. 145.

14. Christopher St. German, *The Power of the Clergy*, ch. 6, cited by Franklin Le Van Baumer, "Christopher St. German," *American Historical Review* 62 (1936/7):646, noted in George Huntston Williams, "The Religious Background of the Idea of a Loyal Opposition" in *Voluntary Associations*, ed. D. B. Robertson (Richmond, Va.: John Knox Press, 1966), p. 62.

15. Williams, "Loyal Opposition," p. 62. Italics in original.

16. George Huntston Williams, *The Radical Reformation* (Philadelphia: Westminster Press, 1962), p. xxvii.

17. Williams notes that a similar theory evolved among magisterial reformers who sometimes sought "parliamentary quasi-conciliar enactment of the royal headship of a national church." Ibid., p. 235.

18. Ibid., p. 176, Cf. pp. 48-49, 77, 78.

19. Ibid., pp. 223, 829.

20. Cadbury, *Book of Miracles*, pp. x-xi. For Boehme, see Jones, *Mysticism and Democracy*, p. 140.

21. Braithwaite, *Beginnings*, pp. xxv-xxvi.

22. Vernon Noble, *The Man in Leather Breeches* (New York: Philosophical Library, 1953). p. 45. See Jones, *Mysticism and Democracy*, pp. 137-138.

23. Braithwaite, *Beginnings*, p. 24. Williams, *Radical Reformation*, pp. 789, 778, 790n. Fox, *Journal*, pp. 30-44.

24. Lloyd, *Quaker Social History*, pp. 24, 1. Jones, *Mysticism and Democracy*, pp. 56, 70-71. Robert Barclay, *Inner Life*, p. 175. Ephraim Pagitt, *Heresiography*, Sixth ed. (London: William Lee, 1662),pp. 101, 233. Cf. added page facing title page. Pagitt inserts Quakers immediately after Seekers, evidently because the two are so closely allied. See also Rufus M. Jones, *Studies in Mystical Religion* (London: Macmillan, 1909), p. 456.

25. Robert Barclay, *Inner Life*, p. 173. Braithwaite, *Beginnings*, p. 45.

26. Braithwaite, *Beginnings*, pp. 44-45. Robert Barclay, *Inner Life*, pp. 273, 255, 175. Fox, *Journal*, pp. 30-46. Jones, *Mysticism and Democracy*, pp. 72-73, 75.

27. Braithwaite, *Beginnings*, p. 12.

28. Pagitt, *Heresiography*, p. 244.

29. Robert Barclay, *Inner Life*, pp. 248-249. Fox, *Journal*, pp. 9, 19-20. Jones, *Mystical Religion*, pp. 411, 414.

30. John Smyth, *Works*, ed. W. T. Whitley (Cambridge: Cambridge University Press, 1915), pp. 275, 277, 271, 269. Williams, *Radical Reformation*, p. 777. William I. Hull, *The Rise of Quakerism in Amsterdam* (Swarthmore, Pennsylvania: Swarthmore Monograph Series, 1938), pp. 12, 3.

31. Abram R. Barclay, *Letters*, p. 285. See also Fox's Letter of 1656 to Friends cited in Fox, *Journal*, p. 282.

32. Smyth, pp. 759, 743-744, 749. Robert Barclay, *Inner Life*, p. 117. Williams, *Radical Reformation*, p. 788.

33. Cf. Williams, *Radical Reformation*, p. 790.

34. "May not the spirit of Christ speak in the female as well as in the male?" George Fox, *Gospel-Truth* (n.p., 1656), p. 81, cited in Hill, *World Turned*, p. 251.

35. Robert Barclay, *Inner Life*, p. 156.

36. John Smyth, *Works*, pp. lxxix-lc; lxxxvii-lxxxix. John Aron Toews, Sebastian Franck: Friend and Critic of Early Anabaptism: (Ph.D. Dissertation, University of Minnesota, 1964), p. 184.

37. Lloyd, *Quaker Social History*, pp. 2-3. Robert Barclay, *Inner Life*, p. 353.

38. Robert Barclay, *Inner Life*, p. 116. This passage is apparently excerpted from a letter from Hugh Bromhead to William Hamerton of London. Harleian MS 360 fol.

39. Agnes L. Tierney, *Ten Studies in the History and Teaching of the Society of Friends* (Richmond, Indiana: Friends Book and Supply House, 1922), p. 13. Braithwaite, *Beginnings*, p. xxv.

40. Jones, *Mysticism and Democracy*, pp. 40-41. Fox, *Journal*, e.g., pp. 10-18.

41. A. S. P. Woodhouse, ed., *Puritanism and Liberty* (Chicago: University of Chicago Press, 1951) pp. 105, 104, 95, 23, 17-19. Bracketed words supplied by Woodhouse.

Bibliography

Early Quakerism

Allen, William. *The Danger of Enthusiasm Discovered in an Epistle to the Quakers.* London: Barbazon Aylmer, 1674.

_____. *A Discourse of Divine Assistance and the Method Thereof.* London: Walter Kettelby, 1693.

_____. *A Persuasive to Peace & Unity Among Christians.* London: B. Aylmer, 1672.

Bainton, Roland H. *The Travail of Religious Liberty.* Philadelphia: Westminster Press, 1951.

Barbour, Hugh. *The Quakers in Puritan England.* New Haven: Yale University Press, 1964.

Barclay, Abram R. *Letters of Early Friends.* London: Harvey and Darton, 1841.

Barclay, Robert. *The Anarchy of the Ranters.* Philadelphia: Joseph Crukshank, 1770.

_____. *Barclay's Apology in Modern English.* Edited by Dean Freiday. Philadelphia: Friends Book Store, 1967.

_____. *Baptism and the Lord's Supper Substantially Asserted.* London: T. Sowle, 1696.

_____. *The Inner Life of the Religious Societies of the Commonwealth.* 3rd ed. London: Hodder and Stoughton, 1879.

Benson, Lewis. *Catholic Quakerism.* Cloucester, U.K.: Derrick P. Faux, 1966.

Braithwaite, William C. *The Beginnings of Quakerism.* London: Macmillan, 1912.

_____. *The Second Period of Quakerism.* London: Macmillan, 1919.

_____. *Spiritual Guidance in Quaker Experience.* London: Swarthmore Press, 1909.

Brinton, Howard. *Friends for 300 Years.* New York: Harper and Brothers, 1952.

_____. *The Religious Philosophy of Quakerism.* Wallingford, Pennsylvania: Pendle Hill Publications, 1973.

Burrage, Champlin. *The Early English Dissenters.* 2 vols. Cambridge: Cambridge University Press, 1912.

Cadbury, Henry J. ed. *George Fox's Book of Miracles.* Cambridge: Cambridge University Press, 1948.

Carroll, Kenneth E. *John Perrot: Early Quaker Schismatic.* London: Friends Historical Society, 1971.

Comfort, William Wistar. *William Penn's Religious Background.* Ambler, Pennsylvania: Upper Dublin United Monthly Meeting of the Religious Society of Friends, 1944.

Edwards, Thomas. *Gangraena.* London: Ralph Smith, 1646.

Ferris, Benjamin. "A Sketch of the Proceedings by Benjamin Ferris." *Delaware History,* April 1968, pp. 30-42.

Flood, James. *A Catholic Critique of the Quaker Doctrine of the Inner Light.* Rome: Gregorian University Press, 1963.

Fox, George. *The Journal of George Fox.* Edited by John L. Nickalls. Cambridge: Cambridge University Press, 1952.

Frost, J. William. *The Quaker Family in Colonial America.* New York: St. Martin's Press, 1973.

Graham, John William. *Psychical Experiences of Quaker Ministers.* London: Friends Historical Society, 1933.

Greenwood, John. *Writings of John Greenwood (1587-1590).* Edited by Leland H. Carlson. London: George Allen and Unwin, 1962.

Guillet, Jacques, et al. *Discernment of Spirits.* Collegeville, Minnesota: Liturgical Press, 1970.

Hill, Christopher. *The World Turned Upside Down.* New York: Viking, 1973.

Hull, William I. *The Rise of Quakerism in Amsterdam.* Swarthmore, Pennsylvania: Swarthmore Monograph Series, 1938.

Hunt, N. C. *Two Early Political Associations.* Oxford: Clarendon Press, 1961.

Jones, Rufus M. *Later Periods of Quakerism.* 2 vols. London: Macmillan, 1921.

_____. *Mysticism and Democracy.* Cambridge, Massachusetts: Harvard University Press, 1932.

_____. *New Studies in Mystical Religion.* New York: Macmillan, 1927.

_____. *Quakerism, A Spiritual Movement.* Philadelphia: Philadelphia Yearly Meeting of Friends, 1963.

_____. *Some Exponents of Mystical Religion.* New York: Abingdon, 1930.

_____. *Spirit in Man.* Stanford: Stanford University Press, 1941.

_____. *Studies in Mystical Religion.* London: Macmillan, 1909.

Kirby, Ethyn Williams. *George Keith.* New York: Appleton-Century, 1942.

Lawrence, Paul R., and Lorsch, Jay W. *Organization and Environment.* Boston: Harvard University Press, 1967.

Littell, Franklin Hamlin. *The Anabaptist View of the Church.* Boston: Starr King Press, 1958.

Lloyd, Arnold. *Quaker Social History.* New York: Longmans, 1950.

148

Loukes, Harold. *The Discovery of Quakerism*. London: Harrop, 1960.

A Loving & Friendly Invitation TO ALL SINNERS TO REPENT AND A WARNING to all backsliders to return unto the Lord, while they have time and space given them, with a brief account of the latter part of the life of John Perrot and his end, &c. London: John Bringhurst, 1683.

Loyola, Ignatius. *The Spiritual Exercises.* Translated by Louis J. Puhl, S.J. Westminster, Maryland: Newman Press, 1951.

McCallin, Joseph A. "The Development of a Legal Theory of Majority Rule in Elections. *Saint Louis University Law Journal* 16 (Fall 1971):1.

Morton, A. L. *The World of the Ranters.* London: Lawrence & Wishart, 1970.

Noble, Vernon. *The Man in Leather Breeches.* New York: Philosophical Library, 1953.

Pagitt, Ephraim. *Heresiography.* 6th ed. London: William Lee, 1662.

Post, Gaines. *Studies in Medieval Legal Thought.* Princeton: Princeton University Press, 1964.

Rahner, Karl. *The Dynamic Element in the Church.* Montreal: Palm Publishers, 1964.

Sewel, Willem. *The History of the Rise, Increase, and Progress of the Christian People Called Quakers.* 3rd ed. Burlington, New Jersey: Isaac Collins, 1774.

Sigmund, Paul E. *Nicholas of Cusa and Medieval Political Thought.* Cambridge, Massachusetts: Harvard University Press, 1963.

Smyth, John. *Works.* Edited by W. T. Whitley. Cambridge: Cambridge University Press, 1915.

Taylor, Ernest E. *The Valiant Sixty.* London: Bannisdale Press, 1947.

Tierney, Agnes L. *Ten Studies in the History and Teaching of the Society of Friends.* Richmond, Indiana: Friends Book and Supply House, 1922.

Tierney, Brian. *The Crisis of Church & State, 1050-1300.* Englewood Cliffs: Prentice-Hall, 1964.

_____. *Foundations of the Conciliar Theory.* Cambridge: Cambridge University Press, 1955.

Toews, John Aron. "Sebastian Franck: Friend and Critic of Early Anabaptism." Ph.D. dissertation, University of Minnesota, 1964.

Tolles, Frederick B. *The Atlantic Community of the Early Friends.* London: Friends' Historical Society, 1952.

Troeltsch, Ernst. *The Social Teachings of the Christian Churches.* New York: Harper & Row, 1960.

Ullmann, Walter. *Medieval Papalism.* London: Methuen, 1949.

Van Etten, Henry. *George Fox and the Quakers.* New York: Harper Torchbooks, 1959.

Vann, Richard T. *The Social Development of English Quakerism, 1655-1755.* Cambridge, Massachusetts: Harvard University Press, 1969.

Weber, Max. *From Max Weber: Essays in Sociology.* Edited by H. H. Gerth and C. Wright Mills. New York: Oxford University Press, 1958.

Williams, George Huntston. *The Radical Reformation.* Philadelphia: Westminster, 1962.

_____. "The Religious Background of the Idea of a Loyal Opposition." In *Voluntary Associations,* pp. 55-71. Edited by D. B. Robertson. Richmond, Virginia: John Knox Press, 1966.

Contemporary Quakerism

Bacon, Margaret H. *The Quiet Rebels.* New York: Basic Books, 1969.

Bartoo, Glenn. "Quaker Decisions." A. M. thesis, University of Chicago, 1952.

Bennis, Warren G., and Slater, Philip E. *The Temporary Society.* New York: Harper Colophon, 1968.

Brinton, Howard H. *Creative Worship.* Wallingford, Pennsylvania: Pendle Hill, 1963.

_____. *Guide to Quaker Practice.* Wallingford, Pennsylvania: Pendle Hill, 1946.

_____. *Reaching Decisions: The Quaker Method.* Wallingford, Pennsylvania: Pendle Hill, n.d.

Brown, A. Barratt. *Democratic Leadership.* London: Allen & Unwin, 1938.

Brown, Thomas S. *When Friends Attend to Business.* Philadelphia: Philadelphia Yearly Meeting, n.d.

Buchanan, James M. and Tullock, Gordon. *The Calculus of Consent: Logical Foundations of Constitutional Democracy.* Ann Arbor: University of Michigan Press, 1962.

Cadbury, Henry J. *The Character of a Quaker.* Wallingford, Pennsylvania: Pendle Hill, 1959.

Carroll, Lewis. *The Annotated Alice.* Edited by Martin Gardner. New York: Clarkson N. Potter, 1960.

Chase, Stuart. *Roads to Agreement.* New York: Harper, 1951.

Clark, Burton R. *The Distinctive College: Antioch, Reed, and Swarthmore.* Chicago: Aldine, 1970.

Collier, Howard E. *The Quaker Meeting.* Wallingford, Pennsylvania: Pendle Hill, 1944.

Dexter, Lewis Anthony. *Elite and Specialized Interviewing.* Evanston: Northwestern University Press, 1970.

Drake, Matthew C. "Quaker Consensus: Helping Learners Understand and Participate in the Quaker Way of Reaching Group Decisions." Ph.D. dissertation, Ohio State University, 1973.

Drucker, Peter F. "A Key to American Politics: Calhoun's Pluralism." *The Review of Politics.* 10 (October 1948):412-426.

Eckstein, Harry. "Case Study and Theory in Political Science." In *Handbook of Political Science,* 7:79-137. Edited by Fred I. Greenstein and Nelson W. Polsby. Reading, Massachusetts: Addison-Wesley, 1975.

Eckstein, Harry and Gurr, Ted Robert. *Patterns of Authority: A Structural Basis for Political Inquiry.* New York: Wiley-Interscience, 1975.

Ellin, Stanley. "An Open Letter to All Friends." *Friends Journal,* January 1, 1976, pp. 10-11.

Falk, Richard A. *Future Worlds.* New York: Foreign Policy Association, 1976.

Futrell, John Carroll. *Making an Apostolic Community of Love.* St. Louis: Institute of Jesuit Sources, 1970.

Goldhamer, Herbert. "Public Opinion and Personality." *American Journal of Sociology,* 55 (1950):346-354.

Hare, A. Paul. "Group Decision by Consensus: Reaching Unity in the Society of Friends." *Sociological Inquiry,* 63 (January 1973):75-84.

Harrison, Paul M. *Authority & Power in the Free Church Tradition: A Social Case Study of the American Baptist Convention.* Princeton: Princeton University Press, 1959.

Hicks, Elias. *Journal of the Life and Religious Labours of Elias Hicks.* New York: Isaac I. Hooper, 1832.

Jonas, Gerald. *On Doing Good: The Quaker Experiment.* New York: Scribner's, 1971.

Jones, Rufus M. "The Sense of the Meeting." In *The Quaker Reader,* pp. 411-415. Edited by Jessamyn West. New York: Viking, 1962.

Keals, John. "There is Something Called Quaker Power. *New York Times Magazine,* March 24, 1968, pp. 56ff.

London Yearly Meeting. *Christian Faith and Practice.* Richmond, Indiana: Friends United Press, 1973.

_____. *Christian Life Faith and Thought in the Society of Friends.* London: Friends' Book Centre, 1943.

_____. *Church Government.* London: Friends' Book Centre, 1968.

McCandless, John H. *Quaker Understanding of Christ.* Philadelphia: Philadelphia Yearly Meeting, 1975.

McGregor, Douglas M. "The Human Side of Enterprise." In *Organizational Behavior and Management,* pp. 452-463. Edited by Donald E. Porter and Philip B. Applewhite. Scranton: International Textbook Co., 1964.

Marshall, Gertrude P. "A View of Representative Meeting: 1952-1975." *Friends Journal,* April 1, 1975, pp. 198-200.

O'Dea, Thomas F. *The Mormons.* Chicago: University of Chicago Press, 1957.

Philadelphia Yearly Meeting (Race Street). *The Book of Discipline.* Philadelphia: Philadelphia Yearly Meeting, 1943.

_____. *Faith and Practice.* Philadelphia: Philadelphia Yearly Meeting, 1972.

_____. *Proceedings and Yearbook of Philadelphia Yearly Meeting, 1976.* Philadelphia: Philadelphia Yearly Meeting of the Religious Society of Friends, 1976.

Pickett, Clarence E. *For More Than Bread: An Autobiographical Account of Twenty-two Years Work with the American Friends Service Committee.* Boston: Little, Brown, 1953.

Pollard, Francis, Beatrice, and Robert. *Democracy and the Quaker Method.* London: Bannisdale Press, 1949.

Rahner, Karl and Vorgrimler, Herbert. *Theological Dictionary.* New York: Seabury Press, 1965.

Rousseau, Jean-Jacques. *The Social Contract.* Translated by Maurice Cranston. Baltimore: Penguin, 1970.

Rowntree, Joshua S. *The Quaker Method of Church Government.* London: Friends Book Centre, 1936.

Shaffer, Blanche W., ed. *No Time But This Present.* Birmingham: Friends World Committee for Consultation, 1965.

Slack, Kathleen M. *Constancy and Change in the Society of Friends.* London: Friends Home Service Committee, 1967.

Smith, Henry Nash. *Virgin Land.* New York: Vintage, 1950.

Steere, Douglas V. *On Speaking Out of the Silence: Vocal Ministry in the Unprogrammed Meeting for Worship.* Wallingford, Pennsylvania: Pendle Hill, 1972.

_____. "The Quaker Decisionmaking Process." Unpublished manuscript of talk given to Guilford College Faculty, February 12, 1975.

Steiner, Jurg. *Amicable Agreement Versus Majority Rule: Conflict Resolution in Switzerland.* Chapel Hill: University of North Carolina Press, 1974.

Trueblood, D. Elton. "The Quaker Method of Reaching Decisions." In *Beyond Dilemmas,* pp. 104-124. Edited by S. B. Laughlin. New York: Lippincott, 1937.

Tucker, Robert W. "Structural Incongruities in Quaker Service." *Quaker Religious Thought,* Autumn 1971, pp. 5-23, 35-40.

Unger, Roberto Mangabeira. *Knowledge and Politics.* New York: Free Press, 1975.

Verba, Sidney. "Assumptions of Rationality and Non-Rationality in Models of the International System." *World Politics.* 14 (1961):93-117.

Von Schulze Gaevernitz, G. *Democracy and Religion.* London: George Allen & Unwin, 1930.

Walker, James F. "The Quaker Meeting for Business." *Pendle Hill Bulletin* 190 (April 1967):1-3.

Webb, Eugene J., Campbell, Donald T., Schwartz, Richard D. and Sechrest, Lee. *Unobtrusive Measures: Nonreactive Research in the Social Sciences.* Chicago: Rand McNally and Company. 1966.

Whitehead, Alfred North. *Adventures of Ideas.* New York: Free Press, 1933.

Wilson, James D. "Quakerism and the Democratic Process." *Quaker Life,* May 1973, pp. 26-29.